Published by New Life Imprints
Christmas The Backstory
©2019 by Christopher R. Berner
Cover Design ©2019 by Ashley Berner
ISBN 978-0-9911023-4-1

NEW LIFE
IMPRINTS

TABLE OF CONTENTS

PART ONE:

Christmas Traditions

THE CHRISTMAS TREE:
A Symbol of Life

Christmas trees. Real, or fake? When do you put it up? And where did we get the idea of having a tree as a part of the Christmas celebration anyway? That's the backstory.

You may not know it, but some claim the Christmas tree should not be a part of a Christian's celebration of Jesus' birth at all, because it started off as part of a pagan ritual. Could be, but the reality is, there's no clear history for the origins of the Christmas tree.

Some claim that in cold climates, where the trees lose their leaves and look lifeless, an evergreen tree was used to symbolize life in the face of the "death" of winter. Not so much a Christmas tree exclusively, but a tree symbolizing life in winter.

There is evidence of trees being used in plays in Europe celebrating creation and the promise of Jesus' coming. Then there's the story of an 8th-century English missionary who saw people about to sacrifice a child in some pagan ritual by an oak tree. He cut down the oak tree and directed their attention toward a nearby evergreen tree as a symbol of life. And some say the great reformer Martin Luther introduced the Christmas tree. By most accounts, the origin of the Christmas tree has its roots in the idea of life – and specifically, everlasting life.

But does it really matter how the tree came to be central part of Christmas? After all, who knows for sure anyway? The real meaning of the tree is found in what we choose to make of it today. So what do we choose to make of it today? What is the biblical perspective on trees? That's the **biblical** backstory.

Trees have been used by people in false religions going back as far as ancient Egypt. Trees have also been used by God from the beginning of time and throughout Scripture. Trees are a symbol of the source of life, or of life in general. But trees are especially used in Scripture for the purposeful, fulfilling, abundant life God wants us to experience.

There's the Tree of Life in the garden (Genesis 2:9). There are trees in the new heaven and earth (Revelation). Psalm 1 describes the blessed man as compared to a flourishing tree. Jeremiah uses trees to illustrate life as well.

> "But blessed are those who trust in the LORD and have made the LORD their hope and confidence. [8]They are *like trees* planted along a riverbank, with roots that reach deep into the water. Such trees are not bothered by the heat or worried by long months of drought. Their leaves stay green, and they never stop producing fruit. (Jeremiah 17:7-8)

Strong, healthy trees are used by God to help us understand what the life He created us for looks like. In Jeremiah, this portrait of a flourishing tree is a symbol for a flourishing life built on a faith relationship with God. It is contrasted with the lives of those who turn their backs on Him.

> This is what the LORD says: "Cursed are those who put their trust in mere humans, who rely on human strength and turn their hearts away from the LORD. [6]They are like stunted shrubs in the desert, with no hope for the future. They will live in the barren wilderness, in an uninhabited salty land. (Jeremiah 17:5-6)

God says that living life apart from Him is like a dried up, dead bush in the heat of the desert. A very graphic contrast is vividly portrayed by these two trees. One is a picture of health, stability, strength, peace, fulfillment, purpose . . . real life! The second is a picture of barrenness, lifelessness, worthlessness, no purpose, no contribution, a sad existence. God wants us to experience life to the fullest in relationship with Him, and He uses a vibrant tree to illustrate what it looks like.

In John 10, Jesus talks about this contrast. He speaks about people who are being robbed of life by their choices. He also speaks of those who find life in Him. But He uses a different illustration. Rather than talking about life using a tree as a picture, He talks about sheep and shepherds. Towards the end of it, he says this:

"I have come that they may have life and have it in abundance. (John 10:10)"

Jesus says that the reason He was born in the manger was to come and bring us life . . . in abundance . . . over the top . . . overflowing! Sounds great, right? That's what God wants for you. You want that, don't you?

To understand the offer Jesus is laying out here, we need to back up and hear His full message of life. And how to find it.

"I assure you: Anyone who doesn't enter the sheep pen by the door but climbs in some other way, is a thief and a robber. [2]The one who enters by the door is the shepherd of the sheep. (John 10:1-2)

[6]Jesus gave them this illustration, but they did not understand what He was telling them. (John 10:6)

So Jesus said again, "I assure you: I am the door of the sheep. [8]All who came before Me are thieves and robbers, but the sheep didn't listen to them." (John 10:6-8)

Jesus isn't the only one trying to get your attention. He's not the only one who wants you to follow or promises that you'll discover life if you do. There are "thieves & robbers" . . . there are people trying to draw you away from Jesus . . . away from life. Jesus is probably referring to the religious leaders of His day. But really, we can have life sucked out of us by so many different people or even things in life.

Today, people, yes, even religious leaders, and the world all around us are promising life through wealth, popularity, partying, or achieving some kind of status or success. In the middle of all this thinking about what life is all about and how to experience a great life – in the middle of all the noise –Jesus says:

I am the door. If anyone enters by Me, he will be saved and will come in and go out and *find pasture*. [10]A thief comes only to steal and to *kill and to destroy*. I have come that they may have *life and have it in abundance*. (John 10:9-10)

What is life all about for you? What are you pursuing? What are the priorities in your life? Be honest. If we looked at how you use your free time, how you use your money, how you interact in relationships with others, what would we conclude is you're living for? Would we quickly conclude that your life is all about Jesus?

Jesus is the one and only giver of life and the only one who can lead us to experience life to the fullest. Everything else is a cheap substitute. Everything!

> "I am the good shepherd. The good shepherd lays down his life for the sheep. (John 10:11)

Here, Jesus hints at the fact that He will sacrifice His life to give life to us. Peter spells it out very clearly – and refers to a tree.

> He himself bore our sins in his body *on the tree*, so that we might die to sins and live for righteousness; by his wounds you have been healed. (1 Peter 2:24)

Jesus sacrificed His life on a tree – the cross – to pay the penalty for our sin, heal our broken, sin diseased hearts, and give us real life.

Through Jesus, the tree represents the provision of real life! Have you placed your faith in what Jesus did for you on that tree? Are you experiencing the abundant life Jesus wants to give you?

As you put up your Christmas tree this year, make it about something more than a nice decoration. Reflect on the wonderful symbol it can be. A symbol of life. Real life. Eternal life. Because Jesus hung on a tree.

This Christmas, every time you see a Christmas tree, take a moment to reflect on the beauty of the tree Jesus hung on to give you life. And commit yourself to live out the abundant life He wants to give you.

What's your idea of life to the fullest? Where does Jesus fit into that picture? He should be in the leading role. What your story is all about.

**Christmas trees remind us that
the Creator of life sacrificed His life
to give us real, abundant life FOREVER!**

DECEMBER 2ND

CHRISTMAS LIGHTS
Finding Light for Life

Who doesn't love a brilliantly lit Christmas tree? Who doesn't love a colorful Christmas light display? Especially if it is choreographed to Manheim Steamroller! Christmas lights are one of the much-anticipated joys and pleasures of Christmas, aren't they? But what's the backstory?

Brilliant and majestic lights were a significant part of Jesus' birth. We all know about the star the wisemen followed. That's the reason we put stars on the top of our trees. Then there was the glorious light display for the shepherds out in the field.

> An angel of the Lord appeared to them, and the glory of the Lord shone around them, and they were terrified. (Luke 2:9)

The brilliant light the shepherds saw was not bright, beautiful stars. It was the radiance of God's glory. The radiance of God's glory filled the area where the shepherds were with light. This same light . . . the glorious, radiant light of the glory of God shined brightly when they left the fields and visited the stable. Why? . . . Because in that manger lay the glorious Son of God who radiated the glory of God in human flesh. No Christmas light display can ever compare with the true Light of Christmas.

John talks about the Light when he gives his account of Jesus coming to earth.

> In the beginning was the Word, and the Word was with God, and the Word was God. [2]He was in the beginning with God. [3]All things came into being through Him, and apart from Him nothing came into being that has come into being. [4]In Him was life, and the life was the **Light** of men. (John 1:1-4)

The light of the stable was not a radiant full moon. It was not a brightly shining star. It was the star of all His-story. It was the radiant light of the Son of God, the true light of Christmas.

The lights we decorate with are beautiful, even spectacular. But they can't compare with Jesus. Jesus is the most brilliant, the most beautiful, the most spectacular light of Christmas. All the other lights of Christmas should inspire us to celebrate Jesus, the light *of life*.

Christmas lights burn out, but Jesus is an eternal light. Jesus is the originator of life, the source of life, and He came to give life. Jesus gives life by giving light – a light that gives us the ability to see the path to life.

> In Him was life, and the life was the Light of men. [5]The Light shines in the darkness, and the darkness did not comprehend it. (John 1:4-5)

"Darkness" here refers to the fallen world of mankind characterized by inability to understand truth, futile thinking, and complete spiritual darkness. John says that the darkness "did not comprehend or overpower it [the Light]" – depending on what translation you read.

In the first sense, "the darkness did not comprehend the light" means that fallen humanity did not **understand** Jesus and what He revealed. In the second sense, "the darkness did not overpower the light" means that fallen humanity cannot **overpower** Jesus and the truth He revealed.

Both translations are supported in other scripture. Perhaps, the lack of clarity is intentional, and it should be translated, "the darkness cannot understand the light, and though it tries, it cannot overpower it."

Man may not understand the light of truth found in Jesus. Man may reject the light of truth. But no power on earth or under the earth can block the light of the world!

Without the light that comes from Jesus, we are naturally in darkness, blind to truth, blind to our sin, blind to our own futility, ignorance, and spiritual death.

Satan, who is the god of this world, has blinded the minds of those who don't believe. They are unable to see the glorious light of the Good News. They don't understand this message about the glory of Christ, who is the exact likeness of God. (2 Corinthians 4:4)

We desperately need light!!

And that light came in Jesus!

For God, who said, "Let there be light in the darkness," has made this light shine in our hearts so we could know the glory of God that is seen in the face of Jesus Christ. (2 Corinthians 4:6)

When you look at the Christmas lights this year, don't just be awed by their beauty. Be awed by the majestic brilliance of the Light of the world. Thank God that He graciously opened your eyes to see the light. Thank God that He made you see His glory in Jesus. Because if He didn't, you would still be in darkness.

Many years after Jesus' birth, we find a fascinating story about light in the gospel of John. Jesus himself affirms John's statements that He is the light and life.

"I am the light of the world" (John 8:12)

Understanding the context and background of this statement reveals that it is both a simple, yet startling and profound declaration.

Jesus' statement took place in the middle of joyous celebration in the lighting of lamps during the Feast of Tabernacles. This feast commemorated God's care of Israel while they lived in tents in the wilderness between Egypt and the Promised Land.
In the Temple treasury where Jesus declared Himself to be the light of the world, stood two giant golden lampstands, on which hung a multitude of lamps, lit after the evening sacrifice. It is said that these lamps would shine light over all the city. The people danced with great

rejoicing around the lamps. Sounds like a great Christmas light display, doesn't it?

Men known for their godliness and good works danced before the crowd with torches in their hands, singing songs and praises. The Levites stood with stringed instruments, harps, cymbals, trumpets and many other musical instruments. The dancing and singing lasted all night till dawn. What a party! A spectacular light display!

Again Jesus spoke to them, saying, "I am the light of the world. Whoever follows me will not walk in darkness, but will have the light of life." (John 8:12)

Jesus alone gives the light that leads us to real life. The Light leads us to see our sins and need of a savior. The Light leads us to confess our sins and repent of our sins. The Light leads us to understand what life is really all about. The Light leads us to the wise and best path for our lives.

As you put up your lights, as you drive around to look at the Christmas lights, celebrate the true light – and life – of Christmas!

Thank and praise God for opening your eyes to see the light. Pray that He will continue to open your eyes to the light of truth. Fight the darkness of human wisdom. Get desperate for God to give you light for your journey through life. Determine to live by the light of God's truth found in His Word.

Celebrate Jesus, the Light of the world! Spread the word of the true light of Christmas!

**You cannot see your way to life
until you chose to follow the Light of life!**

CHRISTMAS ORNAMENTS
Get in the Spirit & Pretty it Up!

The first year my wife and I were going to spend Christmas without either of our children or their spouses was a real downer for me as December approached. I didn't feel like decorating. I didn't even care if we had a Christmas tree. But my wise and godly wife reminded me that the meaning and true celebration of Christmas hadn't changed. And besides, her parents were coming. We had to decorate! I had to refocus and get into the true spirit of Christmas. So we did decorate. And that helped me begin to appreciate the depth and beauty of Christ's birth.

Imagine a Christmas tree without ornaments. Very unusual. And to most of us, not very attractive. We put on ornaments to give it color and character. For some of us the ornaments have specific significance. People visit our homes and admire the decorated tree.

So, what can we learn from our practice of putting ornaments on our Christmas trees? Well, the Apostle Paul says we should "adorn the teaching of God our Savior in everything." (Titus 2:10) This is where the backstory begins.

That word "adorn" is rooted in the idea of bringing something to order. Behind this idea is the realization that something is out of order, not the way it should be. So, steps need to be taken to bring it to the place of order. Things need to be properly arranged as they are meant to be.

The word is also used to describe making something look more attractive such as women, houses, and the temple. (Sorry guys, I guess there's no hope for us!) In more familiar terms, adorning is decorating, prettying up or dressing yourself, or something up. There is a purpose to this. It is intended to make things look more appealing and more desirable. Something that is well decorated draws you in to look more closely.

13

A well decorated Christmas tree draws your attention. You look at the ornaments. You may think about the meaning and significance of some. You might evaluate how the whole arrangement fits together. Maybe there's a common theme that draws you in.

And so it should be with our lives. We are told to adorn the teaching about our Savior in everything. We should make the message of the gospel more attractive, more compelling by the way we live. Jesus talks about how we should attract people to Him.

> "You are the salt of the earth. But what good is salt if it has lost its flavor? (Matthew 5:13)

One of the major uses of salt is to improve flavor. I'm not a huge salt user. In fact, I rarely sprinkle salt on my food. But if the cook didn't put any salt in the pot, the food can be pretty tasteless. Gotta have some salt.

Salty believers will add to and improve the world around them. They make it a more enjoyable place in which to live. How? By being cheerful, kind, and loving. Salty believers will make the world a better place to live in, and this makes the message of the gospel more attractive.

Salt also produces thirst. Salty believers will so demonstrate the beauty of Christ and a sense of meaning and purpose in life that unbelievers will be drawn to Christ by their lives. Certainly not everyone who observes our lives will have an unquenchable desire to have us explain what makes us tick, but some will.

> Be wise in the way you act toward outsiders; make the most of every opportunity. [6]Let your conversation be always full of grace, seasoned with salt, so that you may know how to answer everyone. (Colossians 4:5-6)

Who wants gaps in the placement of ornaments on their Christmas tree? Not me! As you place them, you have to step back every few minutes to make sure they are situated just right. And so it is with life.

We often need to step back and examine ourselves. We need to be alert and wise in how we live. We need to carefully and thoughtfully adorn the gospel because lives are at stake. Paul says we need to make the most of the opportunity we have with those who don't know Christ. This is huge!

So Paul says we need to wisely interact with unbelievers to inject grace into our conversations. This means we are kind and humble in our words. Even if they don't deserve it. We don't tear people down, we bring healing, gentleness, and kindness to the conversation. We speak words that build life in others. Encouragement, blessing, wholeness.

The way we speak should be salty – it should improve the value of the conversation; it should create thirst for more. Yes, we speak the truth, but in a way that is easier to swallow.

We talk about getting into the Christmas spirit. It's the joy, love, and positive vibe many enjoy about Christmas. These characteristics – the Christmas spirit – make Christmas so special. Everyone wants to get into the spirit.

Paul tells us about the positive attitudes and actions that ornament the gospel when we "get into" the Spirit of God. These characteristics of the person who is filled with the Holy Spirit are what make the gospel come alive in real, tangible ways. When people see these, they see the reality of a life changed by Christ. This is what it looks like to adorn the gospel.

> But the fruit of the Spirit is love, joy, peace, patience, kindness, goodness, faithfulness, [23]gentleness, self-control. (Galatians 5:22-23)

This is what shows the reality of Christ within. This is what adorns the gospel:

- **Love**: not just emotion or affection, but *acts* of love. Got it?
- **Joy**: Are you cheerful, happy, positive? Or are you known as a grump, always negative?

- **Peace**: Do you have inner peace because you trust God with your life? Do you generally live in peace with others? Or are you filled with stress and bring stress to your relationships?
- **Patience**: Do you take things in stride? Stay calm? Or do you easily get agitated and irritable. Do you lose your cool quickly?
- **Kindness**: Are you kind in your relationships? Do you do things for others? Are you a giver or a taker?
- **Goodness**: This is moral and practical. Are you primarily good in your character? Do you benefit others? Do people look at you as a good person who is valuable to have around?
- **Faithfulness**: Are you responsible? Do you keep your word? Can people count on you?
- **Gentleness**: Do you choose your words and actions to prevent harm to others? Do you strive to avoid unnecessary hurt even when you have to confront or correct someone? Or are you a wrecking ball? Let's be real. Sometimes when we speak our mind, it only shows there's nothing there of value!
- **Self-control**: Are you impulsive? Is your life well ordered? – not perfect, but also not out of control.

There are more ornaments we can wear to adorn the gospel, but these are some of the first we should put on.

So how about it? Do the people in your life enjoy having you around because you contribute something positive? Would anyone look at your life and say, "I want what she has"? What do you need to do to adorn the gospel by your character? What about in the way you live in relationship with people in your life? Do you adorn the gospel?

This Christmas, don't just put attractive ornaments on your Christmas tree. Put attractive ornaments on your life. And as you put the ornaments on your tree, as you look at them through the Christmas season, let them be a reminder to put on the character of Christ.

Lookin' good?

CHRISTMAS PRESENTS

Giving the greatest gift!

It's supposed to be Jesus' birthday we're celebrating, right? So why do we give presents to each other at Christmas? Love? Because you have to? Duty? Hope for something in return? Buy some favor? Let's be honest, there have probably been times that this was the reality. A gift for your boss maybe?

Fortunately, most times, our motives are way better. We do give Christmas gifts out of love and appreciation. Perhaps it is motivated by sincere gratitude.

But again, how does it make sense that we give each other gifts when it's supposed to be Jesus and His birth that we are celebrating? Actually, it makes perfect sense for us to give to others because Jesus Himself encourages us to express our love for Him by loving others.

Love is at the very heart of Christmas. It was a major motivating factor in Jesus' coming to earth.

> For God so loved the world that he gave his one and only Son, that whoever believes in him shall not perish but have eternal life. (John 3:16)

> This is how God showed his love among us: He sent his one and only Son into the world that we might live through him. ¹⁰This is love: not that we loved God, but that he loved us and sent his Son as an atoning sacrifice for our sins. (1 Jn. 4:9-10)

There are two incredible truths in these verses. First, there is the extent of God's love. God's gift to us in the birth of Jesus was a gift beyond comparison. There was no gift spending limit. All limits were off. It was extravagant. Monumental. Nothing held back. The gift of the eternal Son of God!

Second, there is the manner in which the gift was given. It was a powerful demonstration of God's love **to sinners**. No comparable return gift could be given. Man had no prior love for God that motivated God's gift. And it was not just the gift of God's Son to walk among us. It was the gift of God's Son to die for us!

Have you received that gift? You can't truly give until you first receive God's gift.

The gift of Jesus that we celebrate isn't just about a cute little baby born through unique and intriguing circumstances. It is the gift of a Savior! The gift of forgiveness. Our punishment taken and our sin paid for! God. So loved. The world. You. Me. That He gave His Son.

What do you do with that? How do you celebrate that gift at Christmas? Well, you don't just put up decorations and have a party. You worship. And not just with songs. With your life.

Jesus had many run-ins with the religious leaders of His day. One of the biggest issues of conflict was over religious practice. These leaders were all about religious practices. Their priorities were focused on outward appearance and looking good in public. Jesus shot them down over and over again. When He did, He made it clear that God was intent on a heart relationship with Him, not just religious practices.

> When the Pharisees heard that He had silenced the Sadducees, they came together in the same place. ³⁵And one of them, an expert in the law, asked a question to test Him: ³⁶"Teacher, which commandment in the law is the greatest?" ³⁷He said to him, **"Love the Lord your God with all your heart, with all your soul, and with all your mind.** ³⁸This is the greatest and most important commandment. (Matthew 22:34-40)

It is clear from Jesus' words here that we are commanded to love God with our whole being. It's not just a Christmas thing. Love for God must be the motivating force in our lives in all we do. Love for God must be our foundational purpose, our highest passion, and goal for life. In everything.

This is it. Where it all must begin. Where it all must lead. Where it all must end. This is why you were created. This is what you were created for. This is why you exist!

Love God with white hot passion! With every fiber of your being, LOVE GOD!

DO YOU LOVE GOD?

What can you point to in your life that shows you love God?

The most important gift you can receive this Christmas is the love of God in Christ. Receive his gift of forgiveness – of life!

And the most important gift you can give this Christmas is to love God. Give your heart to him, commit your life to honoring him, loving him.

But what about giving gifts to others?

When Jesus was asked about the greatest commandment, He stated that it is to love God with all we've got. But then, He continued:

> The *second is like it*: *Love your neighbor as yourself.* (Matthew 22:39)

Apparently, when John heard this teaching of Jesus, he got it. After describing the magnitude of God's love, he says:

> Dear friends, since God so loved us, we also ought to love one another. (1 John 4:11)

Why didn't Jesus stop with: "Love God"? Why didn't John stop with telling us about the incredible love of God? Because there is a direct connection between loving God and loving others. John makes it clear that you can't truly love God without truly loving the people in your life!

> God showed how much he loved us by sending his one and only Son into the world so that we might have eternal life through him. ¹⁰This is real love-- not that we loved God, but that he loved us and sent his Son as a sacrifice to take away our sins. ¹¹Dear friends, since God loved us that much, we surely ought to love each other. (1 John 4:9-11)

> This is how we know what love is: Jesus Christ laid down his life for us. And we ought to lay down our lives for our brothers. ¹⁷If anyone has material possessions and sees his brother in need but has no pity on him, how can the love of God be in him.

[18]Dear children, let us not love with words or tongue but with actions and in truth. (1 John 3:16-18)

The more you appreciate the love of Jesus, the more you will actively love Him. When your heart is filled with love for Jesus, your heart will be filled with love for others that will motivate you to action. When you actively love Jesus, you will actively and sacrificially love others. If you don't have a heart to love and bless others, you don't have a heart to love and bless Jesus.

If people judged my love for Jesus by how they see me loving others, what would they conclude?

This Christmas, don't just do the gift giving thing out of habit. First, focus on the incredible gift of love given to us in the person of Jesus. Consider all He did in coming until it fills your heart with love and passion to give yourself more fully to Him. Then, give to others as an expression of your love for Jesus. Love them as Jesus has loved you. After all, that is the best gift you can give.

CHRISTMAS CHILD

Giving Sacrificially

The drama of the Christmas story is so full of wonder, isn't it? A **very** pregnant mom making a **long** journey with her husband. The struggle to find a place to sleep. A baby born in a stable.

For those of us who know the back story, it's even more wonderful. This baby is the gift of God from heaven. This baby is the result of amazing generosity and sacrifice.

And this wasn't the only amazing birth. Remember Mary's cousin Elizabeth, her husband Zechariah, and their son John? Luke tells us that "Elizabeth was not able to conceive, and they were both very old." But, she did in fact have her own miracle baby. More back story. More drama. We'll get to some of that.

The story of Jesus and children doesn't end there either. We see children showing up later in Jesus' life. How fitting because children have a special place in God's heart. And God cares very deeply about how we treat children.

One of the most well known and loved stories of Jesus' life involves His encounter with some children. When others would ignore children and even try to keep them away from Jesus, He warmly welcomed them.

> And whoever welcomes one child like this in My name welcomes Me. [6]"But whoever causes the downfall of one of these little ones who believe in Me-- it would be better for him if a heavy millstone were hung around his neck and he were drowned in the depths of the sea! (Matthew 18:5-6)

When Jesus says to "welcome" children, he is saying we need to receive and accept them, give a warm embrace, treat them as valuable. He tells us to do this, "in my Name" – on His behalf, as He would. He is calling us to be His hands and feet. To love children as He does. To treat children as He does.

What does that mean? It means we show them they matter. It means we are gentle, compassionate. We care for them. We look out for them. Just like Jesus. Did you see what Jesus said about those who don't do right by children? This is serious business!

It's really no surprise that we see this coming from the heart of Jesus. The Old Testament is full of commands to care for the less fortunate. Orphaned children get special attention from God, and He is very serious about His people caring for orphaned children.

> A father to the fatherless, a defender of widows, is God in his holy dwelling. (Psalm 68:5)

> Defend the weak and the fatherless; uphold the cause of the poor and the oppressed. (Psalm 82:3)

> Learn to do good. Seek justice. Help the oppressed. Defend the cause of orphans. Fight for the rights of widows. (Isaiah 1:17)

> Pure and genuine religion in the sight of God the Father means caring for orphans and widows in their distress and refusing to let the world corrupt you. (James 1:27)

There are many, many more verses that demonstrate God's special compassion toward vulnerable and neglected children. God is specifically described as a father to the fatherless. And He takes this role very seriously. He commands, yes, **commands** us to defend and care for the fatherless. We are given the responsibility to care for orphans in their distress.

So, what does all this have to do with Christmas? Glad you asked! I've heard people say several times that Christmas is for the children. What they mean is the children in their own life. Children of family and friends. And most times, the idea is that Christmas is all about our kids getting nice gifts and being happy. It's all about the joy the adults get as they fawn over the children when they open their gifts.

Sorry, do I seem a bit cynical? Well, maybe just a bit. Really, I always enjoyed giving gifts to my children and watching them open them. But Christmas isn't all about the children. It's all about one child, Jesus. And there were times when I thought the gift giving might be squeezing that focus out of Christmas.

We did work hard at keeping the focus on Jesus at Christmas. Still, I couldn't help but think that we spent way too much money on things that weren't worth it. And my thoughts would gravitate toward children who didn't have parents to love on them and give them gifts at Christmas – or any time for that matter. Children that have a special place in the heart of God.

Maybe we need to expand our efforts to see children experience love and joy at Christmas. What if we put some effort into blessing those children God cares so much about? There are millions of hurting children around the world. And many in our own communities.

Let's get practical. Here are some ways you can share the love, hope, and message of Christmas with a hurting child.

1. **Your Local Church:** If your church has a program for ministering to hurting kids, this is a great place to get plugged in. Talk to your church leadership. No program? No problem! Start one.

2. **Operation Christmas Child:** Operation Christmas Child is a ministry of Samaritan's Purse. "It is a global program facilitated through hundreds of thousands of trained volunteers. Local believers in more than 100 countries deliver Operation Christmas Child shoebox gifts, present the Gospel, and facilitate our follow-up discipleship program, The Greatest Journey."
   https://www.samaritanspurse.org/what-we-do/operation-christmas-child/

3. **Prison Fellowship's Angel Tree:** "Every child has a story. For 2.7 million children in the U.S., that story may be filled with the abandonment, loneliness, and shame that come from having a mom or dad in prison. Angel Tree® reaches out to the children of

prisoners and their families with the love of Christ. Every Angel Tree parent's family is also given access to a free, easy-to-read copy of the Bible (available in English or Spanish)."
https://www.prisonfellowship.org/about/angel-tree/

4. **Make it personal:** Find a single mom or dad who is struggling. Buy them and their kids gifts and invite them to join you in your Christmas celebrations. Consult with your church or local organizations to find someone to bless if you don't know anyone.

These aren't the only ideas, and you may have a better one. But may I encourage you, find one. The more personal, the better. Get the whole family involved. Just remember, always try to share the message of the gospel in whatever you do. What an opportunity to show love and share Christ!

Christmas is all about *the* child. Jesus.

What better way to celebrate *the* Child than to bless a child this Christmas?

DECEMBER 6TH

CAROLS
Celebrate Jesus!

Singing Christmas carols has been a significant tradition for many people for many years. I grew up singing lots of carols year after year. We sang carols in Sunday school, in church, in children's and youth meetings, in school, and we even went to malls to sing carols. As a teen, I remember our youth group going around the neighborhoods to sing carols. (One time someone offered our youth group a bottle of wine after singing. Figure that one out.) They are played on the radio and in the malls. They are often sung and recorded by people who show no interest in the Savior they sing about. They really are a major part of Christmas.

So, what's the backstory of carols? Well, there is pretty solid agreement that the singing of Christmas songs dates back to 129 AD. The earliest songs were written in Latin and weren't called carols. Some suggest they grew out of the winter solstice celebrations. Where did the name "carol" come from? Again, it is unclear. Some say it has Latin origins, others, French, and still others, English. Francis of Assisi and Martin Luther get credit for furthering the singing of carols. Most of the carols we sing today were written in the 1700s with a few coming from the 1800s.

I have sung all the standard carols so many times, I know every line from memory. I don't have to think about it. You know how it goes, you're singing along and then you realize you been singing every word perfectly while you've been thinking about something totally different – a Christmas gift, a party, whatever. My guess is we've all been there.

Many people absolutely love Christmas carols and can't imagine Christmas without them. But maybe carols aren't your groove. I get it, I prefer contemporary music – it's what I best connect with and how I most genuinely worship. So, I like modern arrangements of carols with added lines that focus on worship and praise directed toward God. I love contemporary Christmas songs.

Here's the thing. The point is not whether we sing carols – whether traditionally or in a contemporary style. The point is also not that we abandon carols and just sing contemporary Christmas worship songs. These issues don't matter to God. God doesn't have a preferred style of worship. God has a preferred style of heart.

Worship played a significant role in the birth of Jesus. Mary praised God when she visited Elizabeth. The angels praised God when they announced the birth of Jesus to the shepherds. The wisemen worshiped as they presented their gifts to Jesus. They would have worshiped in different ways, probably mostly without a melody, almost definitely without instruments. But it was worship. Genuine worship. And that is the key.

You may recall the time Jesus met with a Samaritan woman by a well. In the course of conversation, she asked Jesus about worship. This woman was concerned about *where* and *how* you worship. Jesus focuses on the *heart* and *who* you worship. She's all focused on the proper *place* and *practice* of worship. Jesus says God is focused on the right *attitude* and *accuracy* of our worship.

> But the time is coming-- indeed it's here now-- when true worshipers will worship the Father in spirit and in truth. The Father is looking for those who will worship him that way. [24]For God is Spirit, so those who worship him must worship in spirit and in truth." (John 4:23-24)

The worship God is looking for is worship that is in spirit and truth. God desires authentic worship. God desires worship that is more than just saying words or singing songs. He wants us to really mean it. He wants worship that is genuine; worship that comes from the heart! In fact, though God deserves, desires, and commands worship, He is actually opposed to superficial worship – singing songs just because we like them or out of ritual.

26

The sovereign master says, "These people say they are loyal to me; they say wonderful things about me, but they are not really loyal to me. Their worship consists of nothing but man-made ritual. (Isaiah 29:13)

Can it get any clearer? God isn't interested in our singing Christmas songs just because we enjoy it. God's not impressed by our singing when our hearts aren't filled with genuine appreciation for Him and what He has done.

Now this isn't to say that if we are enjoying worship we aren't genuinely worshiping. It doesn't mean that if we feel something or are expressing ourselves emotionally in worship that it isn't the real deal. God wants us to love – and worship – with our whole being, heart soul, mind, and strength. So, every part of who we are should be engaged in worship. Worship should involve our thinking, emotions, affections, and yes, even our bodies. We should be all in when it comes to worship. God deserves it! But in all of this, it must be about worshiping and praising God. God must be the focus.

Maybe some of the activities – even church activities – that surround the celebration of Christmas actually distract us from celebrating Jesus. Could it be that much of it is just focused on the fun and feeling of the Christmas spirit rather than the Savior? Do we lose the focus on Christ in it all? Have we lost the true wonder of His birth so that our worship is more religious practice than real, authentic worship?

If you really get the wonder and significance of Jesus' birth, you will get a heart filled with worship. When you come to appreciate how incredible it is that Jesus left heaven and came to this messed up world, lived among messed up people, and then took our punishment, you will have a humbled heart that is expressed in worship and praise. That's what God is after.

There's another important principle Jesus pointed out to the Samaritan woman. It is that God desires accurate worship. Worship is not just about singing and music, it is about worshiping God, and so our worship must be focused on things that are accurate and true about God. Every word of our Christmas worship doesn't have to be about some deep theological mystery, but it must be theologically correct. It doesn't need to be expressed in flowery or complicated poetry, but it must be true to the Word of God. It's not about the style of the song, but it is about the message of the song. The truth and the message should be clear. So we should focus on the message of the songs as we sing them. Let the truths expressed capture your thoughts – and your worship.

This Christmas, can we determine to be engaged in authentic worship? No, that doesn't mean you have to sing carols. It doesn't mean you have to sing contemporary Christmas songs. It's really not about the style at all. Don't let it be about that. If it is, you've probably stopped worshiping. You may be worshiping a style rather than the Savior in a manger.

Don't let it be about getting into the "Christmas spirit" and warm fuzzies. That's a superficial and a sad substitute for responding to the move of the Spirit of God, leading you to authentic, meaningful worship.

Don't let it be about enjoying the season and feeling good about life. Make it about enjoying your Savior and rejoicing in Him.

Don't let the activities and business of Christmas steal the wonder, joy, and worship of Jesus' birth from your heart.

Fight to keep your mind and heart focused on Him.

Commit yourself to genuine worship.

CHRISTMAS COOKIES

Connecting for Christ

Christmas cookies. Many of us can't imagine Christmas without them. Fresh out of the oven, or even days later, we enjoy chocolate chip, ginger, oatmeal raisin, sugar, and many other types of cookies as a delicious Christmas tradition. Sometimes with coffee. Sometimes with milk. How about right now?

How did we get to be so consumed with the consumption of cookies at Christmas? What's the backstory?

The tradition of Christmas cookies seems to have started in the Middle Ages in Europe. They started out as simple, plain biscuits. Then, as spices and refined sugar became more available, the revolution began to give us some of the cookies we enjoy today.

Back then, people would bake large amounts of cookies to be prepared for the guests that were sure to show up during the Christmas season. Sound familiar? Another tradition was to give cookies as gifts, sometimes accompanied by some other homemade craft. Again, pretty familiar to many of us. Who hasn't been a beneficiary of the Christmas cookie exchange?

You can probably recall times of sitting around with other people enjoying a variety of Christmas cookies. Maybe after a meal at a home. Maybe with the neighbors. Maybe at church or in the break room at work. Does it really matter? Christmas cookies are just fun to eat and fun to share.

It's interesting that the whole backstory of Christmas cookies started out with a focus on sharing, giving, and enjoying them with others, that has continued to this day. Cookies certainly are about the flavor, but the social aspect is also very much alive today. That's a **really** good thing at Christmas or any time. Why? Because life is all about relationships.

Christmas really is a great time to evaluate and build our relationships. Maybe this Christmas we can gain some insight and skills that can make the whole season more meaningful in our relationships. Maybe Christmas cookies can play a part in that. Wouldn't that be great?

In Scripture, we find a strong emphasis on relationships. Remember, we've already explored Jesus' statements that the two greatest commandments are to love God and love others. Relationships.

But, there's so much more – the **specifics** of what it looks like to love others. One of the common ways we can explore these specifics is by looking at the "one anothers" of the New Testament. These are verses that use this phrase or idea to describe how we should act in relationships with others, primarily fellow believers. These principles could revolutionize our relationships. And again, what better time to heal and improve the relationships in your life? Maybe this Christmas can be different.

> Show family affection to one another with brotherly love. Outdo one another in showing honor. (Romans 12:10)

> Instead of being motivated by selfish ambition or vanity, each of you should, in humility, be moved to treat one another as more important than yourself. ⁴Each of you should be concerned not only about your own interests, but about the interests of others as well. (Philippians 2:3-4)

> Encourage one another and build each other up. (1 Thessalonians 5:11)

Family love – the kind of family love we know should be part of every family – should characterize our relationships. It's appreciating others, caring for them and their well-being. It involves respect and honoring them. Our focus in our relationships should be on serving, making the lives of others better. Encouraging them. Building them up. It's about putting their interests, desires, and goals first – before ours. Good relationships are built on becoming great at the dance of competing desires. And you start by letting go of your agenda to serve theirs.

What if this Christmas, we repurposed our relationships and made it all about them instead of all about me? What kind of cookies do **they** like?

> Live in peace with each other. (1 Thessalonians 5:13)

> So then, let us aim for harmony in the church and try to build each other up. (Romans 14:19)

Live at peace. Live in harmony. If we are experiencing conflict, this may seem impossible. But maybe, just maybe if we baked some Christmas cookies and shared, it could get better.

I know. That sounds so corny. But it's not. Really! Put the repurposing principle to work. Start serving them. And, maybe as you share some cookies together you can really try to **listen**. Listen to **their** issues. Listen to understand. Seek first to understand, then to be understood. Try to put yourself in their shoes. Try to understand how **they** feel. Then, speak words that heal, rather than words that hurt. Is it really worth fighting over? Let it go!

> Therefore, accept each other just as Christ has accepted you so that God will be given glory. (Romans 15:7)

> Be completely humble and gentle; be patient, bearing with one another in love. (Ephesians 4:2)

> So let's stop condemning each other. (Romans 14:13)

How did Christ accept you? Yeah, with all your bumps and blemishes! You weren't even close to perfect. God accepted you **by** grace, **with** grace. So why do we put such a heavy load of expectations on others?

We want people to be patient with us. We don't want people to jump all over us when we make mistakes. We want patience. We want the benefit of the doubt. So, why don't we give what we want? You don't have to say something about every mistake or failure – unless you're going to lift them up with encouragement.

> So confess your sins to one another and pray for one another so that you may be healed. (James 5:16)

> And be kind and compassionate to one another, forgiving one another, just as God also forgave you in Christ. (Ephesians 4:32)

Confession is good for the soul. It's also good for relationships! Step up. Stop trying to hide. Be honest. Then, humbly ask for forgiveness. Strong relationships are built when we own our errors and make it right.

How did God forgive you? Completely. Permanently. Without you deserving it in any way. Knowing you would do it again. "Forgive one another, just as God also forgave you in Christ." Their sins against you can never compare to your sins against God. It's time for you to forgive.

Strong relationships that endure the pain of brokenness are built on the commitment to choose forgiveness.

Relationships are the fiber of life.

We can't avoid them.

If we want to honor the birth of our Savior, we have to get serious about having God-honoring relationships.

What can you do to improve your relationships this Christmas?

Bake some cookies!

PART TWO:

Key Players

RAHAB & BATHSHEBA

Sinners Welcome!

Labeled. For life. At least that's what people put on us. Rahab – *the harlot!* Bathsheba – *the adulteress!* Labeled! Forever. Until Jesus.

Yes, Rahab was a prostitute. But she acted in faith and helped the Hebrew people gain victory over the city of Jericho. In fact, she's listed among the great people of faith in Hebrew 11. Yes, Bathsheba did sin with King David. But she became the mother of King Solomon. And both of these ladies with a "past" appear in the family line of . . . Jesus! Check it out in Matthew chapter one.

The family line of Jesus teaches us a lesson we see all through Scripture. The person most broken by sin can become most beautiful in the Savior.

Jesus' encounters with people who were broken by sin always come down to the same thing. Jesus put no limits on the sin or the sinner that could be forgiven. When Jesus saw repentance, He always offered forgiveness and restoration. In fact, Jesus preferred the "sinners" over the religious leaders of His day. In fact, He told them, "I assure you: Tax collectors and prostitutes are entering the kingdom of God before you!" (Matthew 21:31)

No sin is beyond the reach of God's forgiveness. No sinner is beyond the reach of God's grace. No person is beyond the reach of God's love. The person most corrupted by sin can become most useful to the Savior. Jesus loves taking people who are broken by sin and restoring them to the beauty they were created for.

Who are you? How do you view yourself?

For many of us, our view of ourselves is shaped by how we think others see us and what they think of us.

How do **you** think of yourself in terms of your identity?

Some people think of themselves in terms of the past. What I did or didn't do in the past. Past successes or more often failures. So, some people are trapped in a box of who they were in the past. It's a box they can't seem to break free from. And this box keeps us from seeing and finding joy in who we really are in Christ.

Some people think of themselves in terms of the future. What I am planning to do. Who I am planning to become. Who I dream of being. Who I wish I was now. Some people are trapped in the box of "who I hope I'll be in the future." It's a box that is a tyrant, always pushing us to try harder, while telling us we'll never get there. We'll never be who we want to be.

Some people think of themselves in terms of the present. Who I am now. If I feel like I am doing ok, I feel good about myself. When I fail or don't perform as well as I think I should, I feel bad about myself. Often our view of ourselves in the present is linked with what we believe others think of us. It's also linked to how we think we compare with others. But it can also just be how we see ourselves.

Some of us are trapped in this box of our present view of ourselves based on our performance, how we measure up to others, and how we believe others think of us. This box gets us trapped in discouragement and hopelessness. I won't try to achieve much because I don't have much to achieve with. What can I do?

Sometimes we get trapped in all three boxes at the same time. We believe our past failures determine who we are and who we can become. We don't have much hope of getting to where we want to be in the future. So we drift and feel defeated in the present.

All of this thinking just messes us up. All of these boxes are manufactured by Satan.

These are lies.

These thoughts ignore what we can become when we put our faith in Christ.

All these thoughts ignore what Jesus does for us when we are given new life by faith in him.

All these thoughts keep us from embracing who we are in Christ.

> Therefore, if anyone is in Christ, he is a new creation; the old has gone, the new has come! (2 Corinthians 5:17)

Paul talks here about those who are "in Christ". What does this mean? It means that when we put our faith in Christ, we are immediately united with Christ by faith in His work on the cross. What Christ accomplished on the cross becomes your accomplishment. Christ defeated sin and death, and Christ's payment for sin is payment for your sins by faith in Him. Christ completed a life of perfect righteousness, and Christ's righteousness and perfection are yours by your faith in Him. Christ's life is yours. That's the glorious exchange that takes place when we trust Christ.

> God made him [Christ] who had no sin to be sin for us, so that in him we might become the righteousness of God. (2 Corinthians 5:21)

Paul describes this as becoming a "new creation". Something new has begun. It's not just a change in destiny and behaviors or the old cleaned up and made a little better. No, it is a whole new life –a whole new way of living. The moment you put your faith in Jesus, God started something new in your life, something He promises He will finish.

> And I am certain that God, who began the good work within you, will continue his work until it is finally finished on the day when Christ Jesus returns. (Philippians 1:6)

A new you was birthed the day you put your faith in Christ and God has promised that this new you will continue to develop until you are made completely like Jesus.

Paul is not finished with his incredible description of you. He says, "the old has gone." The old is the past life along with what characterized life before coming to Christ – the old way of living and approaching life. This is not a statement of theory; this is a statement of fact.

On top of all this, Paul says a new life has come! When we come to be "in Christ" by faith in Him, a new life – a new way of life begins. In Romans 6, Paul states this same idea of the old life ending and a new life beginning:

> We know that our old sinful selves were crucified with Christ so that sin might lose its power in our lives. We are no longer slaves to sin. [7]For when we died with Christ we were set free from the power of sin. [8]And since we died with Christ, we know we will also live with him. (Romans 6:6-8)

Just like Rahab and Bathsheba, the great women of faith, God redeems my past – I am not defined by who I was. So this Christmas I will believe that I am who God says I am.

I will stop seeing myself and acting based on anyone's opinion of me except God's.

I will believe and act on what God says about me, that I am a new person in Christ and God is growing me up in this new life.

I will choose to live my life in keeping with who I am in Christ, not who I was before Christ.

When I blow it, I won't believe the lie that this is who I am, and I am hopeless to change because I know I have new life in Christ, and I will change.

This Christmas, will you join Rahab and Bathsheba as part of Jesus' story of the broken made whole?

**The person most broken by sin
can become most beautiful in the Savior.**

JOSEPH

Portrait of a Righteous Man

When you think about people who are central figures in the events surrounding Jesus' birth, certainly Joseph will come to mind. We all know the basic role Joseph plays in the story, but there's so much to the backstory that we need to understand.

To get the full significance of Joseph's actions in the story, we have to understand a bit of Jewish customs. Many cultures have a practice of engagement where two people agree to marry. It's not meant to be broken, but it's usually not considered binding in any way either. Later a ceremony makes the marriage official.

So, you probably already knew all that. What's the point? The point is that we need to understand that Jewish engagements were different in several ways. Most importantly the engagement was far more serious. In fact, it could only be broken by a formal divorce for cause. Now we can jump into the Christmas story.

> This is how Jesus the Messiah was born. His mother, Mary, was engaged to be married to Joseph. But before the marriage took place, while she was still a virgin, she became pregnant through the power of the Holy Spirit. (Matthew 1:18)

In our world today where biblical morality is so commonly ignored, we don't immediately understand the seriousness of this situation for Joseph. He was engaged to a young lady that he thought was morally pure – a virgin. Now, he finds out she's pregnant. Her honor was destroyed. She's made a mockery of him and their engagement. His honor was teetering on the edge of a cliff. This could ruin his life in many ways. What is he to do?

There was only one thing to do. A formal divorce was necessary. And of course, everyone needs to know very clearly that he's NOT the father! Make this thing a public announcement so everyone knows the facts. He must protect his honor and reputation.

That would be the expected backstory of Joseph's thinking. But, that's not how it went.

> Joseph, her fiancé, was a good [righteous] man and did not want to disgrace her publicly, so he decided to break the engagement quietly. (Matthew 1:19)

Perhaps you're familiar with the story and so you saw that coming. But remember, familiarity can lead us to miss something significant. Joseph was definitely within his rights to break off the engagement. Most people from his family and friends would expect it. But Joseph was a good man. He loved Mary. Even though he had every reason to think she betrayed him, he still loved her and wanted to protect her from public disgrace. He decided he would try to keep the whole situation as quiet as possible. Don't go around telling everyone about it. Don't bad mouth her. Take the hits that might come by protecting her.

Now, who does that? Not too many. Most of us, put in a situation like this, would respond quite differently. We'd be talking to everyone, telling them about what was done to us. How we were betrayed. How hurt we are. We would definitely want to make sure everyone knows we're the innocent person in all this! I'm not going down with you!

But Joseph was good man. A righteous man. A decent, honorable man. Wow! What an example for us!

> As he considered this, an angel of the Lord appeared to him in a dream. "Joseph, son of David," the angel said, "do not be afraid to take Mary as your wife. For the child within her was conceived by the Holy Spirit. 21And she will have a son, and you are to name him Jesus, for he will save his people from their sins." 22All of this occurred to fulfill the Lord's message through his prophet: 23"Look! The virgin will conceive a child! She will

give birth to a son, and they will call him Immanuel, which means 'God is with us.'" (Matthew 1:20-23)

Mind officially blown! An angel? "Don't be afraid to marry Mary." "What? You knew my plans? How did you know that?" A bit unnerving! "A child by the Holy Spirit?"

Let's stop right there. We know the whole story. But just put yourself in Joseph's position, hearing this. This has never happened before! A baby, that came from the Holy Spirit?!? I think I would have had some real questions on that one. And, would I have believed it? Am I only dreaming? Well yes, I am dreaming, but this isn't like any other dream. This so real!

And there's a backstory within the backstory. The angel tells Joseph this is a fulfillment of prophecy. I wonder if this was the tipping point for Joseph. Maybe he recalled the prophecies of a virgin giving birth to a son who would be "Immanuel, God with us." Maybe this isn't so crazy after all. Joseph got the message very clearly.

When Joseph woke up, he did as the angel of the Lord commanded and took Mary as his wife. (Matthew 1:24)

Well, that sounds simple. Wake up. Do what the angel told you to do. If only it was always that simple for us.

Don't miss the magnitude of Joseph's obedience here. Remember the whole public shame issue. Remember the questions that still must have lingered in Joseph's mind.

But maybe, we don't have to understand it all to obey. Could we be like Joseph and just simply obey because God is God and we're not? What if we chose to obey God even though we don't know how everything is going to end up? What might God be able to do in our lives? Through us?

The story of Joseph's obedience and character is not finished here. He's still got two more powerful lessons to teach us. He married Mary. But...

But he did not have sexual relations with her until her son was born. And Joseph named him Jesus. (Matthew 1:25)

Now why did Joseph and Mary abstain from sex until Jesus was born? And why did Matthew feel it necessary to tell us this? If this wasn't Scripture, this would definitely be way too much information! And it's highly unlikely Matthew tells us this just as an aside.

While we can't be sure why Joseph and Mary abstained from sex, there is a lot of agreement on the probabilities. First, this abstinence would remove any doubt of the virgin birth. They were more concerned with integrity and removing any doubt of the baby's identity than they were in personal pleasure. Second, it is suggested that there may have been deep reverence for the baby that would have kept them from engaging in sex. The reality is that it was perfectly acceptable, but out of their desire to honor God's plan, they refrained. What determination to do the right thing!

So, what can we take away from all this digging into the backstory of Joseph's life? We are reminded that obedience is always the right choice even if it doesn't make sense or makes us uncomfortable.

Like Joseph, we will be faced with choices in life where obedience to God will mean taking a step of faith. We know the right thing to do, but don't know how things will end up. Obedience is always the right call.

There will be other times when we will be sure that obedience will mean we take some hits. No matter how much we think it will hurt, obedience is always the best path to take.

How are you doing with practicing obedience in your life? Will you be like Joseph? Will you determine to choose obedience?

What a great gift to give Jesus this Christmas!

ZECHARIAH

One of the good ones.

Religious leaders. They don't always have the greatest reputations or character. We've heard of the scandals over and over again. We may know of a few first hand. Moral failures are common. Pride, abuse of authority and power, greed – way too familiar. And it was that same way when Jesus was born.

Here's the backstory. The priests of Jesus' day were known for their self-righteous attitudes and pride. They made the rules. They enforced the rules. They looked down on others who didn't keep the rules like them. They had position, power, and attitude to match. Enter Zechariah. One of the few good ones.

> In the time of Herod king of Judea there was a priest named Zechariah, who belonged to the priestly division of Abijah; his wife Elizabeth was also a descendant of Aaron. ⁶Both of them were righteous in the sight of God, observing all the Lord's commands and decrees blamelessly. (Luke 1:5-6)

Zechariah isn't that well known or talked about around Christmas. He's kind of in the shadows of the story. Part of the backstory. Add his wife Elizabeth to the conversation, and we might remember him. But it seems he would be perfectly happy with playing a backstory role.

Luke tells us that Zechariah was a priest who was righteous. He was blameless in terms of obeying God. This doesn't mean he was sinless. It means that when he did sin he didn't ignore it. He didn't try to cover it up. He acknowledged his sin and repented.

And right there, we encounter the first, powerful challenge from this backstory guy. It comes to us in the form of a question: "Would God point to me as blameless?" Wow! What a sobering question! Am I committed to obedience? When I blow it, am I quick to admit my sin, confess it to God and others as needed? Do I practice genuine repentance that leads to change? Is there something, anything, that I am overlooking? Ignoring? Covering up? Let's be honest. Because we're not hiding anything from God, anyway!

As we dig deeper into this backstory, Luke says that Zechariah was not just righteous and blameless in the eyes of men like the other priests, He was righteous before God. **God** saw him as righteous! (Way more important!)

We can put on a show. Try to look all spiritual and holy before others. Sing the carols. Go to the Christmas events celebrating Jesus. Do all the good religious things that make us look good to the other people at church. But our hearts can be empty. It's just what we do at Christmas. And we have to do it, otherwise people will notice and talk about us.

Or maybe, just maybe, we could be like Zechariah (not the other priests) and be real. What if we determined that we won't be just religious people who do religious things for show? What if this Christmas we chose to focus on the real meaning and purpose of Christmas?

Don't just be religious this Christmas. Make it real. Don't let it be about all the activity – even religious activity. Determine to put your heart into it.

Back to Zechariah and Elizabeth. Blameless. Obedient. Honoring God from their hearts. But . . .

> But they were childless because Elizabeth was not able to conceive, and they were both very old. (Luke 1:7)

That drops heavy. Especially in that culture where everyone wanted children. Not having children caused great disappointment and even disgrace. Not having children equaled not being blessed by God. And why not blessed by God? Well, there must be sin in your life. God is punishing you. That's what a lot of people would think.

But wait, we know those people would be wrong! This wasn't punishment. This wasn't the withholding of God's blessing because of some failure. God makes it clear that this couple was **blameless**.

But isn't that the way people go? . . . "It must be because of something in your life!" And don't we sometimes buy into that thinking. When something goes wrong, don't we easily question, "What did I do to deserve this?"

What an encouragement this story is. It totally blows that common thinking out of the water! It makes it clear that just because something bad happens in our lives doesn't mean it's God's punishment.

Sure, we should examine ourselves and be sensitive to the ministry of the Holy Spirit to see our sin, confess, and repent. But don't get crazy. Don't get hyper-critical and down on yourself. Don't assume there must be something you're missing.

Are you living in guilt this Christmas? Maybe guilt that has been there for years. Guilt over sin you've already dealt with before God. Guilt other people have put on you. Or guilt over some sin you assume must be there because life hurts?

It's time to embrace God's mercy and forgiveness. If you have put your faith in Christ and what He did on the cross to take your punishment and pay the penalty for your sins, you are forgiven.

> God made you alive with Christ. He forgave us **all** our sins.
> (Colossians 2:13)

No matter what you've done. There is forgiveness in Jesus. God is not punishing you for what you have done. There can be lingering consequences due to some sins, but God is there with His gracious favor to help you deal with them. He doesn't want these consequences to hold you back. He wants to use them as part of your story of His grace and empower you to rise above them. Embrace forgiveness. Embrace grace.

Zechariah's place in the backstory of Christmas isn't finished. One day, when he was serving in the temple, an angel appeared to him and promised him that he and Elizabeth would be having a baby! And not just an ordinary baby, this baby was to play a critical role in God's plan. His name? John. John the Baptist. Whoa!

Sometimes God's blessings come at the most unexpected times. That sure was the case for Zechariah and Elizabeth. They had waited a long time. Probably gave up on having a child long ago – surrendered that dream to the sovereign plan of God. Then it happened. In the most amazing series of events. A miracle baby.

What are you waiting for? What is the Christmas gift you wish – you pray – God would finally give to you? Don't stop praying, but surrender it to the sovereign plan of God while you wait.

Your miracle might be coming. It may not be exactly as you expect. It may not be when you expect. You may come to the place where you realize you don't need or even want that miracle any more. No matter what, you can know that God has a plan. It's a perfect plan rooted in perfect knowledge and wisdom.

There's so much more we can learn from Zechariah. I've left out the end of the story. It's quite amazing. You can read it in Luke 1. I get a good laugh out of God's answer to Zechariah's request for a sign that this was for real. Check it out.

This Christmas, will you embrace the lessons of this backstory? Will you embrace truth and reject the lie that you only suffer because of your faults and failures? Will you fully embrace the forgiveness given to you in Jesus? Will you continue to trust God for whatever miracles He has in store for you – whether it's the miracle you are praying for, or the miracle of grace to endure? What will be your backstory this Christmas?

JOHN – SON OF ZECHARIAH

All About Jesus!

The common portrait of Zechariah's son John, better know as John the Baptist, is one of a fiery preacher declaring his message of repentance and baptizing people at the Jordan river. And this is part of the story. But there's much more to who this man was. His backstory starts a few months before his second cousin Jesus is born. We'll pick up the backstory at the point where Mary goes to visit her cousin Elizabeth right after she has been told that she will give birth to Jesus.

> A few days later Mary hurried to the hill country of Judea, to the town ⁴⁰where Zechariah lived. She entered the house and greeted Elizabeth. ⁴¹At the sound of Mary's greeting, Elizabeth's child leaped within her, and Elizabeth was filled with the Holy Spirit. (Luke 1:39-41)

It's so easy to move quickly past this when you read the entire story. But this is really cool and profound. We considered this before but need to go back to it.

John – unborn and still in his mother's womb – expressed joy in the presence of Jesus who was still in His mother's womb. John worshiped Jesus before either of them were born! Can't fully get my head around that one. Here is yet another reminder that Christmas is about worshiping Jesus.

Who was this kid? The backstory is this. Back in the time of the Old Testament prophets, Isaiah declared that there would be a great prophet who would come and announce the coming of the Messiah.

> Listen! It's the voice of someone shouting, "Clear the way through the wilderness for the LORD! Make a straight highway through the wasteland for our God! (Isaiah 40:3)

Matthew, Mark, and Luke all state that Isaiah was referring to John. John himself affirmed his understanding that God had sent him ahead of Jesus to fulfill this prophecy. When the religious leaders asked him who he was, he replied,

> "I am a voice shouting in the wilderness, 'Clear the way for the LORD's coming!" (John 1:23)

John had one purpose. To declare the coming of the Messiah. Everything in his life was focused on this task. It shaped his view of himself, and his view of Jesus.

> John testified about him [Jesus] when he shouted to the crowds, "This is the one I was talking about when I said, 'Someone is coming after me who is far greater than I am, for he existed long before." (John 1:15)

John was all about exalting Jesus. That was his passion, declaring the message of Jesus as the Messiah, calling people to repentance, pointing them to Jesus. He did it before he was born, and he continued it till the day he died.

Do you know who was born first, Jesus or John? John, by about 6 months. So, why is he saying that Jesus "existed long before" him? Because John understood the true identity of Jesus. Central to John's message was that Jesus was eternal God, come to earth to bring redemption. John was all about the gospel.

> John told them, "I baptize with water, but right here in the crowd is someone you do not recognize. [27]Though his ministry follows mine, I'm not even worthy to be his slave and untie the straps of his sandal." (John 1:26-27)

John was on the scene first. By birth and in ministry. He could have pulled seniority, protected his territory, tried to keep the attention of the people on himself. But he didn't. In fact, he totally humbled himself. He had such a high regard for Jesus, such a deep appreciation for Jesus, he didn't even feel worthy to take off Jesus' sandals! Humble adoration.

Passion to honor Jesus. Directing all attention to Jesus. And – get this – he was the fulfillment of prophecy. Not a small thing!

> The next day John saw Jesus coming toward him and said, "Look! The Lamb of God who takes away the sin of the world! (John 1:30)
>
> He must become greater; I must become less." (John 3:30)

What was John's single focus in life? Declaring Jesus' coming. Preparing the people for Jesus' coming. Why was he so passionate about it? Why all the self-denial? Why was he so intent on stepping into the background to give Jesus the spotlight?

Because he knew – and he wanted everyone to know – that Jesus is "the Lamb of God who takes away the sin of the world." He knew there was a Savior who would die to pay the penalty of man's sin. He knew this Savior was man's rescue from eternal punishment. He knew he had to get the word out. Lives were at stake. And Jesus deserved every man's worship.

John the Baptist is referred to as the "forerunner." The meaning of this is that John came as the one who would go before Jesus to prepare the way for Jesus by preparing the people to receive him. That was his mission.

That's pretty much our mission too. It's not so much that we are to prepare people for the coming of Jesus on the scene in person, but we are to represent Jesus in a similar way. John was the forerunner, we are ambassadors.

> Everything is from God, who reconciled us to Himself through Christ and gave us the ministry of reconciliation: [19]That is, in Christ, God was reconciling the world to Himself, not counting their trespasses against them, and He has committed the message of reconciliation to us. [20]Therefore, we are ambassadors for Christ, certain that God is appealing through

us. We plead on Christ's behalf, "Be reconciled to God." (2 Corinthians 5:18-20)

Each of us who have embraced Christ as our Savior – without exception – have been assigned two jobs in this passage. We have been given the ministry or responsibility of sharing the message that man can be reconciled to God through Christ. To put it another way, we have been given the responsibility to share the message of the gospel to those around us.

If you're a Christian, this is your job, your responsibility. You can't ignore it. It has been given to you by God. You can't pass it off on someone else (like your pastor), it has been given to you, personally.

The second job we've been given is to be ambassadors for God. You know what it means to be an ambassador? It means we must be conscious of representing God 24/7. It means we aren't about positioning ourselves and promoting our agenda in this foreign land. No, we must, at all times, function in our role as ambassadors, promoting God and His agenda. This is a very serious position, and responsibility. But, remember, lives are a stake!

This Christmas, remember that little baby that worshiped Jesus before he was even born. Take to heart the example John set for us as he grew up with a laser-like focus on representing Jesus, pointing people to Jesus.

Then, let's embrace the responsibility God has given us to share the message of the gospel. Let's represent Him well as His ambassadors, committing ourselves to honoring Him in our dealings with people.

Christmas is a time when many people
are far more open to talking about Jesus.
Let's seize this great opportunity!

DECEMBER 12TH

THE INNKEEPER

Giving Jesus the Leftovers?

In those days Caesar Augustus issued a decree that a census should be taken of the entire Roman world. [2](This was the first census that took place while Quirinius was governor of Syria.) [3] And everyone went to their own town to register. [4]So Joseph also went up from the town of Nazareth in Galilee to Judea, to Bethlehem the town of David, because he belonged to the house and line of David. [5]He went there to register with Mary, who was pledged to be married to him and was expecting a child. [6]While they were there, the time came for the baby to be born, [7]and she gave birth to her firstborn, a son. She wrapped him in cloths and placed him in a manger, because there was no guest room available for them. (Luke 2:1-7)

Wait. That's not how I remember the story. Where's the part about Mary and Joseph going from place to place looking for a room? Where's the part about the rude, insensitive innkeeper? In fact, where's the inn? What corrupt translation is this?

Don't get your knickers in a bind! Let me explain. The reality is that the backstory that most of us are familiar with is just not in the Bible. No where in the Bible can you find any account of Mary and Joseph looking for a place to stay. That's right, no knocking on doors and getting turned away till finally they get to stay in the barn. And no, there is no innkeeper in the Bible. In fact, the word "inn" is really very misleading if not a complete error when you look at the Greek word in is translated from. (So yes, the title of this chapter is inaccurate.)

The Greek word translated "inn" in some translations occurs only 2 other times in the New Testament. The two other times are in Mark 14:14 and Luke 22:11. In both of those places, it is the "guest room" where Jesus and his disciples ate the Passover meal together. Jesus also uses another Greek word to refer to this room which means "upper room." An upstairs room, set aside for guests, was a common feature of homes. And, to make this understanding more certain, there is another Greek word that more clearly refers to a commercial inn.

So, it seems very clear that this was a room in a regular house. A room set aside for guests. But it was already occupied – probably to overflowing by family members who had traveled in like Joseph & Mary for the census. So, they had to stay in the area downstairs that was where the animals were kept. That's the backstory.

But this doesn't change the fact that there was no room for them. But, why was there no room for them? Couldn't someone have given up their space The homeowner? Some of the other relatives there as guests? After all, Mary was obviously pregnant! Wouldn't you think someone would be willing to give up their comfort for a pregnant woman?

Nope. Didn't happen. They were comfortable, safe, warm and secure. We love our comfort. So Joseph, Mary, and Jesus got the leftovers.

But let's not be too hard on the relatives for not giving Jesus a place to be born. They wouldn't have known that Mary was giving birth to the Messiah. So, maybe they should get a little break on that one. But still.

And what about us? We know. We know who Jesus is. We know the place He deserves in our lives. And still, all too often, we give Jesus our leftovers.

The leftovers of our time.
The leftovers of our energy.
The leftovers of our money.

We have our agenda.
We have our task list.
We have our shopping lists and financial goals.

And once we've got all that in order, then we can give Jesus some space. Well, that is if there's anything leftover.

Am I off the mark? Is this not you? If not all the way down the line, at least in some areas some of the time? Not you? Great. Stop here.

Still with me? Yeah, me too. I struggle with this.

It's so easy to get caught up in our little world, our desires, goals & plans. It's so ingrained in us. Drives me nuts sometimes! Paul talks about his struggle in Romans 7. James talks about our desires that wage war within us in James 4. The struggle is real. Too real. And the messages that come at us every day stoke the fires of this pursuit of self-gratification.

In the thick of all this, God's Word is very clear. It's clear about the dangers of boxing Him out. And it's clear about what we should be living for. It's so clear we try not to think about what it really means. You probably know the verses, but read them again with a view to seeing how your life measures up.

> "Don't store up treasures here on earth, where moths eat them and rust destroys them, and where thieves break in and steal. 20Store your treasures in heaven, where moths and rust cannot destroy, and thieves do not break in and steal. 21Wherever your treasure is, there the desires of your heart will also be. (Matthew 6:19-21)

> Seek the Kingdom of God above all else, and live righteously, and he will give you everything you need. (Matthew 6:33)

> Do not love this world nor the things it offers you, for when you love the world, you do not have the love of the Father in you. 16For the world offers only a craving for physical pleasure, a craving for everything we see, and pride in our achievements and possessions. These are not from the Father, but are from this world. (1 John 2:15-16)

But those who desire to be rich fall into temptation, into a snare, into many senseless and harmful desires that plunge people into ruin and destruction. (1 Timothy 6:9)

Why is the "pursuit of more" so dangerous? Why does God give such serious warnings and tell us not to live for having more money or more stuff? Because the way material things and money work, we rarely feel like we have enough! So it becomes an endless pursuit. We always "need" more. God gets boxed out. Jesus gets the leftovers. And too often, there's little if anything leftover.

If getting more is a focus of my life . . .
If getting more is a priority of my life . . .
If I have my heart set on a little more . . .

THEN . . . .
Jesus doesn't have my focus.
Jesus isn't my highest priority.
Jesus doesn't have my heart.

I will not be a good manager of what God has given me.
I won't be generous in giving to God.
I won't be generous in helping others.
I won't have energy or time for God.

Investing into God's kingdom and impacting people for eternity suffers greatly when I'm living for a little more.

So I need to do a check-up. How much of my resources are invested into furthering Christ's kingdom? Do I skip my time with God, skip church, skip church activities, skip giving, because my life is spent on other things?

Does Jesus get the living room or the spare room in your life?
What place will Jesus have in my life? Will He get the leftovers this Christmas?

THE PEOPLE OF BETHLEHEM

Distracted

> But you, O Bethlehem Ephrathah, are only a small village among all the people of Judah. Yet a ruler of Israel will come from you, one whose origins are from the distant past. (Micah 5:2)

Bethlehem lies 5-6 miles south of Jerusalem, sitting about 2,400 feet above sea level. It was the location of the story of Ruth, King David's great-grandmother. It was also the birthplace of David. Micah's prophecy tells us that it was small and insignificant at the time of Jesus' birth. But with all the people traveling to Bethlehem because of the census order, it had probably ballooned in the number of people there when Jesus was born.

So, where were they when Jesus was born? It's interesting that there is no mention of the people of Bethlehem and all the census-tourists in the Bible. Now, just because something is not mentioned in the Bible doesn't mean it didn't happen. But, was anyone else there? It seems that there would be at least a brief mention of them if they came to offer congratulations and see the new baby. What would have kept them away?

There are actually some very easy answers to why the people in Bethlehem might not have visited Jesus. Remember what's going on. A lot. With probably hundreds of extra people in town, there would be quite a bit of extra activity. There would have to be arrangements for lodging and meals. And of course, this was all way more complicated back then. No supermarkets. No microwaves. Plus, there would be so much catching up to do with family you haven't seen in a very long time. And, I can almost hear the talk . . .

> *"Did you hear that Jacob had so many relatives show up he had to put the couple from Nazareth in with the animals? And,*

Rebekah says the young woman was with child! (Well, they are from Nazareth any way. Nothing good comes out of Nazareth!) Oy vey! Stay away from that house!"

I have quite an imagination sometimes, but I think that very well could be close to what might have happened. Certainly, there would have been plenty to keep people busy. And distracted.

Maybe, when you drill down to the backstory, that's the common thread woven through the story of the people in Bethlehem. There was just a lot going on, who could blame them for missing the birth of the Messiah? They were busy and distracted. Give them a break, right?

Yes, there are times when there's so much activity that things we would normally notice get overlooked. There are times when we just don't have time for some of the things we see as important in life. Chores get skipped. No time for family dinner. Can't make the kid's game. Not gonna make it to the live nativity, sorry. You know the drill.

But, what if hours of business become days and then weeks and months. What if years go by and we are still too busy for what matters most? It happens. Way too often.

I remember a time when I was working two different ministry jobs, one at church and one as a hospice chaplain. One evening while I was working at home, we had a discussion with our son about staying home and not going out with his friends so much. His reply? "Well dad, you're always working anyway." Wow! That hurt. Mostly because it was true. At that very moment, I knew something had to change. I had to free up some time for my family. I couldn't lose my son!

Yeah, there's so much to draw us away from what matters most. Our jobs, home improvement, everyday chores, entertainment, volunteering, and yes, ministry.

For example, you remember Martha and her sister Mary when Jesus came to visit. What happens when we get too caught up in activity?

Let's look closer at Martha and see. Let me just remind you of how it went in Luke 10:38-42 – with a little creativity thrown in.

Luke tells us that Jesus and His disciples are traveling to Jerusalem, and they stop at the home of their friends Mary and Martha. Realize this was almost definitely unannounced. What woman at that time wouldn't be frantic? Quick, tidy up! Throw those clothes in the closet! Put those dishes away! They need to be fed. Better get cooking. Jesus and His disciples are here. Everything must be perfect. So much to do. Mary! Where's Mary?

Are you kidding me! Mary is in the living room just laying off! And Jesus is just sitting there talking and isn't even encouraging her to help me! Unbelievable. "Lord! Does this seem fair? I'm doing all the work and Mary's just sitting here! Tell her to help."

Did you notice she starts out calling Jesus "Lord" but ends up telling Him what to do? That's one of the things that often happens when we get wrapped up in our personal agenda and what we want to do in life. We become bossy. We tell others what to do so we can facilitate our plans. We might even get bossy with God, like Martha. People become a means to an end, a tool for us to use to get what we want. We stop caring about what other people want or what's good for them. We can become demanding, controlling, and manipulative. All because we have our agenda, our plans, and we are determined to get it done.

And if they don't get in line with our program, we become irritable, rude, and judgmental. Isn't that what we see in Martha? She's obviously upset. She's judgmental of Mary and rude to Jesus. And we can be the same way.

Now here's the thing. It isn't always something bad that gets us this way. What was Martha doing? Something good. Some of us would have sided with Martha if it weren't for what Jesus said. Maybe you would have been right there with Martha. Trying to get a nice meal on the table for Jesus and the gang. Just trying to be a servant! And Mary's just not willing to sacrifice and do ministry. Have you heard something like that? Have you *said* something like that?

Here comes Jesus into the mix. "My dear Martha, you are worried and upset over all these details! There is only one thing worth being concerned about. Mary has discovered it, and it will not be taken away from her." (Luke 10:41-42)

Well that was unexpected. You would think Jesus would encourage Mary to join Martha in sacrificially serving. Had Jesus never heard one of those sermons?

Jesus says there is only one thing worth being concerned about. What is it? It's what Mary was doing. Sitting with Jesus is more valuable than serving Jesus. In fact, you can't serve Jesus properly if you don't sit with Jesus properly. Ministry can be the enemy of relationships.

But perhaps there is something even deeper here to learn. What was Martha doing? She was frantically preparing a big meal and trying to get everything else in order. Her "ministry" was about external, physical things, not spiritual matters. Mary was investing her time and energies into fellowship with Jesus. Learning from Him. Growing closer to Him.

So what can we take away from all this to make Christmas more meaningful this year? For starters, we can be alert to the negative impact of filling our lives with activity – especially at Christmas when there's so much activity going on. But it goes beyond Christmas as well. We would do well to examine our lives and make corrections to assure that we are investing our focus, time, and energies into what matters most, knowing Jesus and making Him known.

How are you doing with sitting at the feet of Jesus? Are you a person whose life is characterized by intimate fellowship with Jesus? Are you taking time to pour into the lives of others to help them grow?

Might your child say you're too busy for them? Friends? Family? Are you more like Martha, or Mary?

SHEPHERDS

Outcasts are in the Cast!

Today we look at one of the most familiar passages of Scripture telling the story of Jesus' birth. You may have read it many times. You may have even memorized it at some point in your life. I want to encourage you to read it once again, attempting to interact with it with fresh eyes. Picture it and try to experience it as if you were there.

> In the same region, shepherds were staying out in the fields and keeping watch at night over their flock. [9]Then an angel of the Lord stood before them, and the glory of the Lord shone around them, and they were terrified. [10]But the angel said to them, "Don't be afraid, for look, I proclaim to you good news of great joy that will be for all the people: [11]today a Savior, who is Messiah the Lord, was born for you in the city of David. [12]This will be the sign for you: you will find a baby wrapped snugly in cloth and lying in a manger." [13]Suddenly there was a multitude of the heavenly host with the angel, praising God and saying: [14]Glory to God in the highest heaven, and peace on earth to people He favors! [15]When the angels had left them and returned to heaven, the shepherds said to one another, "Let's go straight to Bethlehem and see what has happened, which the Lord has made known to us." [16]They hurried off and found both Mary and Joseph, and the baby who was lying in the feeding trough. [17]After seeing them, they reported the message they were told about this child, [18]and all who heard it were amazed at what the shepherds said to them. [19]But Mary was treasuring up all these things in her heart and meditating on them. [20]The shepherds returned, glorifying and praising God for all they had seen and heard, just as they had been told. (Luke 2:8-20)

How unexpected! A very ordinary night. Some very ordinary guys sitting out in the fields with their sheep. Probably swapping stories, gossip, jokes. Huddled around a fire? Yep, just like every other boring night. And then, all glory broke loose!

The story of Jesus' birth is actually all about events in the lives of very ordinary people. Common people like Mary and Joseph, Zechariah and Elizabeth, Simeon, Anna. The innkeeper and the people of Bethlehem – not much notoriety there.

Sure, there was a miraculous conception, but then it seems a very ordinary – perhaps we should say sub-ordinary – birth of a baby. There were no medical professionals. No soft bed. No boiled water (that we know of. Apparently, no mid-wife. No crib. It would seem, not even any family to welcome baby Jesus. Just Mary and Joseph in a barn. Spectacular!

And then comes the public announcement of Jesus' birth. Let's announce the birth of the king! A king's birth deserves nicely printed announcements. Certainly, the town criers in all the nearby towns will be declaring the celebration 24/7. Oh yes, he must have a celebration to top all celebrations! And all the well known people will attend and bring their gifts. Everyone will dote on the baby and talk about how he looks like his mother. Hmm. No resemblance to his father. This will be so exciting!

No. Jesus birth was announced . . . to shepherds . . . shepherds?!?!? Well yeah, at least there were angels and an angelic choir to make the announcement. That was super cool. But still, they appeared to shepherds. Out in the field. Where only the shepherds would see it.

Really? Why shepherds? In the field? Why not the mayor or the town council in the public square? Or at least someone of some popularity, some respected position in the town of Bethlehem?

Maybe you don't get why this is such a big deal. Let's dig into the backstory of shepherds.

Most Bible scholars agree that shepherds spent most of their time in the fields, with other shepherds, away from everyone else. They had no influence, no place in the community. They were the blue-collar laborers, unnoticed, if not ignored by everyone. Shepherds were in the lower classes of society.

So why shepherds? Why not someone more respectable? Isn't it strange how an event that was so significant involved so many simple, insignificant people? They were insignificants that became significants in the plan of God. God specializes in using ordinary people to accomplish extraordinary things.

In Scripture, we see many people with no status who were used by God in significant ways:
- Abraham – a tent-dwelling nomad.
- Joseph – despised by brothers, sold as slave, an ex-con.
- Moses –As a member of the Egyptian royal family, he was the enemy!
- Rahab – a prostitute!
- Gideon – a frightened, timid farmer.
- Amos – farmer, shepherd.
- Daniel – teenager.
- Mary – young lady, probably a teen.
- Joseph – carpenter.
- Disciples – fishermen, hated tax-collector, uneducated.

No aristocrats here. No power brokers. No rich and famous. No educational elites. Just ordinary people who were willing to join God in His plan to change the world!

Do you feel like a nobody? Christmas teaches us that God takes nobodies and makes them somebodies in His glorious plan. Isn't that just the way God works?

> Remember, dear brothers and sisters, that few of you were wise in the world's eyes or powerful or wealthy when God called you. [27]Instead, God chose things the world considers foolish in order to shame those who think they are wise. And he chose things that are powerless to shame those who are powerful. [28]God chose things despised by the world, things counted as nothing

at all, and used them to bring to nothing what the world considers important. God specializes in using ordinary people to accomplish extraordinary things. (1 Corinthians 1:26-28)

God takes people's lives full of sin and failure, people who don't have position, or status, or great abilities. He leads them to repentance, forgiveness and redemption. He chooses them. He empowers them. He works through them to accomplish great things for His glory.

God takes people with a past and turns their lives around to do great things through them in the present, and lead them to a glorious future.

God wants to take your ordinary and make it part of His extraordinary. God wants to take your mess and turn it into a miracle of grace.

Jesus' birth proves to us that God doesn't need great people to accomplish great things in this world for His glory.

God accomplishes significant things through insignificant people.

In Jesus, the insignificant become significants.

Now that's something to celebrate this Christmas!

DECEMBER 15TH

HEROD

Dealing with Evil

As I sit there here this morning, my wife and I are refugees. Just over two months ago we evacuated after going through one of the worst hurricanes in history. Our island in the Bahamas and our home were devastated by hurricane Dorian. It was quite a traumatic event for many people whose lives were devastated. Their homes were heavily damaged or flattened. Every business in town was wiped out. And hurricane Dorian didn't just affect the lives of ungodly people, people who were evil or rebellious toward God. Dorian ripped through the lives of good people, godly people who love the Lord, people who had committed their lives to serving Him. How does this make sense? How do you make sense of devastation like this? And certainly, there are other situations in life where it's so difficult for us to figure out what in the world is God doing. Life threatening disease, financial ruin, relationships torn apart by betrayal, a rape, murder, our homes robbed of everything of value.

How do we make sense of these things when all we've been doing is trying to honor God and serve Him? This question certainly would have arisen in the hearts and minds of people in Bethlehem after the birth of Jesus.

Soon after Jesus was born, Roman soldiers invaded this little town of Bethlehem and began systematically and ruthlessly going from home to home murdering babies. Does it get any more evil than this? How do you make sense of such horrific events?

The backstory of this unthinkable evil lies at the feet of King Herod. King Herod (Herod the Great) was a ruthlessly cruel, paranoid, jealous and power-hungry ruler. He murdered anyone he thought might threaten his authority. He even killed several members of his own family!

You recall that after the wisemen met with Herod, inquiring where Jesus, "the King of the Jews" would be born, Herod was furious. He was determined to keep any king from taking his throne.

> Then Herod, when he saw that he had been outwitted by the wise men, flew into a rage. He gave orders to massacre all the male children in and around Bethlehem who were two years old and under, in keeping with the time he had learned from the wise men. (Matthew 2:16)

That's part of the backstory of the murder of helpless babies, but the backstory of the horrific events in Bethlehem goes even deeper. To get some insight into how something like this could happen, how evil could touch the lives of good decent people, we have to go back to the Old Testament. And what we find is that this event was actually prophesied.

> Then what was spoken through Jeremiah the prophet was fulfilled: [18]A voice was heard in Ramah, weeping, and great mourning, Rachel weeping for her children; and she refused to be consoled, because they were no more. (Matthew 2:17-18)

This prophecy is a bit clouded by the reference to Ramah and Rachel, but there is enough to clearly see that God said this massacre of babies would happen. Matthew is clearly stating this.

Now we could discuss and debate God's role in this horrific event. Did God just see that it was going to happen and told His prophet? Did God just allow it? Or, did God actually plan or orchestrate it? These are deep issues of theology. But in the end, is it not true that the sovereign, all powerful God of all creation could have prevented this? Or stopped it? Sure He could.

How do we make sense of all this? The story of babies being slaughtered is a pretty negative Christmas story if we don't have anything else to give us some perspective on this.

And this is not the only time we see such evil in Jesus' story. After Herod the Great died, his son Herod Antipas took over. He had John the Baptist beheaded. He shows up in some startling verses in Acts 4.

> The kings of the earth took their stand and the rulers assembled together against the Lord and against His Messiah. [27]"For, in fact, in this city both Herod and Pontius Pilate, with the Gentiles and the people of Israel, assembled together against Your holy Servant Jesus, whom You anointed, [28]to do whatever Your hand and Your plan had predestined to take place. (Acts 4:26-28)

It was the single most evil series of acts in all of history. No comparison. Jesus was falsely accused and given a fake trial set up to find Him guilty no matter what it took. He was savagely beaten. He had a crown of thorns pressed into his scalp. Then, he suffered an agonizing death by crucifixion. Because God had planned it. God had determined and decreed long before that this would happen. Exactly the way it happened.

There's so much we don't understand in all this. In fact, there is so much we just *can't* understand. And that's the first reality we need to embrace as we try to find something to help us make sense of evil in the world.

> "My thoughts are nothing like your thoughts," says the LORD. "And my ways are far beyond anything you could imagine. [9]For just as the heavens are higher than the earth, so my ways are higher than your ways and my thoughts higher than your thoughts. (Isaiah 55:8-9)

When it comes to understanding what God is doing as He orchestrates history, we have to realize the God thinks and acts on a level we can never understand completely. We could argue that what happened in Jerusalem when Jesus was crucified was just wrong and find fault with God for it. We could argue that what happened in Bethlehem when babies were killed was just wrong and find fault with God for it. We can argue that things that have happened in our own lives were wrong and find fault with God. But our reasoning is faulty. God's is perfect. We *can't* understand it. All we can do is humbly accept that God is always right in all He does.

That brings us to the second reality we must understand in this. God is sovereign over evil, and evil people. He is sovereign over all of history, past, present, and future.

> The LORD has made the heavens his throne; from there he rules over everything. (Psalm 103:1)

> He does as he pleases with the powers of heaven and the peoples of the earth. No one can hold back his hand or say to him: "What have you done?" (Daniel 4:35)

No evil can interfere with God's plan. Evil will always fail to change or stop what God is doing. We must choose to accept this by faith.

The third reality is that if God allows evil, it is for a purpose. God is a God of purpose. God is working His plan to fulfill His purpose in history.

> I declare the end from the beginning, and from long ago what is not yet done, saying: My plan will take place, and I will do all My will. (Isaiah 46:10)

So, here are the 3 realities for facing evil:
1. We can't understand it all. We must trust that God is wise and right in all that He does.
2. God is sovereign over **everything**. **EVERYTHIING!**
3. God has a purpose and a plan. It is **always** the best plan. Believe it. Still struggling? Repeat realities 1-3.

In the face of evil, here is the beauty of Christmas we can celebrate: Jesus came to change the hearts of evil people and begin the process of doing away with evil. That will continue until He comes again to eradicate evil completely and forever. Jesus will have the final word over evil. Celebrate that present and future hope this Christmas.

SIMEON

Led by the Spirit

Now here's a real backstory guy. Recognize the name. No, we're not talking about Joseph's brother in the Old Testament. We meet this Simeon at the temple, eight days after Jesus' birth.

> Now there was a man in Jerusalem called Simeon, who was righteous and devout. He was waiting for the consolation of Israel, and the Holy Spirit was on him. [26]It had been revealed to him by the Holy Spirit that he would not die before he had seen the Lord's Messiah. [27]Moved by the Spirit, he went into the temple courts. (Luke 2:25-27)

Sometimes biblical descriptions can be so brief, but so profound. If we pause to stop and really think about what is said, it can be quite powerful and challenging.

Luke describes Simeon as righteous and devout. Being righteous, Simeon was a man characterized by **doing** right. He was obedient to God. Consistently. He was a man of godly character and integrity.

And here is another challenge from a backstory guy. As we look at these backstory people, this description, this model keeps showing up. And each time, we are challenged to compare the portrait of our lives with theirs. Would anyone describe me as righteous? I don't know, but God help me to be that person! Don't you want that to be an accurate description of your life?

But there's a second word used to describe Simeon: "Devout." We use that word sometimes. "She's a devout Christian." "He's a devout Muslim." This English word is pretty accurate in translating the Greek. It carries the ideas of being sincere, serious, devoted, conscientious, and committed. This isn't someone who's half-hearted, complacent, sometimes in, sometimes out.

This is a person who is all in. They don't play church. They are actively living the life. God isn't just a part of their life. God is what their life is all about. The center. The focus.

For them, Christmas isn't just a holiday. There's something more, something deeper, more profound. Christmas is celebrated in the heart, not just the mall, the kitchen, or in front of the TV watching the latest Hallmark Christmas movie. Nothing wrong with those things. Those things are enjoyed. It's just that there's something more. Much more. It's being devout, not just doing it because that's what people do.

What would a "devout" Christmas look like for you? What can you do to make it happen?

The next thing Luke says about Simeon is that he was an expectant waiter. No, He didn't serve table at a restaurant with hopes of getting a good tip. (Sorry, dad joke) Simeon was, "Waiting for the consolation of Israel." He was waiting for the promise of the Messiah to be realized. He knew He would someday meet the Messiah. God had made that promise to him (v. 26). So he waited. And waited. And waited.

Sometimes in life, we have to wait on God's perfect timing for the realization of the promise. It's actually a pattern we see repeated many times in Scripture. Abraham and Sarah waited 25 long years from when God first promised a son until Isaac was born. Isaac had to wait 20 years for a child. Jacob worked 7 years for Rachael. Joseph waited about 13 years to go from slavery to the palace. Joshua and Caleb had to wait for 40 years to get into the promised land. David had to wait 16 years after he was anointed to *be* king, until he actually took the throne *as* king. Israel waited **hundreds of years** for the coming of the Messiah.

Waiting is a very real part of God's plan. And we hate it! Right? It's one of the hardest things to do. But each of these stories teach us how to wait. We must wait with patience. Confident hope. Trust. Faithfulness. For Simeon, the waiting had to be hard. Israel was oppressed under the authority of Rome. No independence. Religion was all about ritual and was filled with hypocrisy and corruption. And still, Simeon held firmly to the hope of Israel's consolation.

But what is this "consolation"? It is the Greek noun *paraklesis*, "comfort, consolation" and comes from the word *parakaleo*, to come alongside to help, encourage, comfort. Jesus calls the Holy *Paraklete (John 14:16)*.

There's more to the idea of what this consolation was all about. Redemption, rescue from oppression, and freedom were key. But I just love the connection with the terminology used to refer to the Holy Spirit. This consolation is connected to the comfort and encouragement that we get when God comes alongside. God came near in the person of Jesus to comfort, encourage and to help us in our most desperate need.

Whatever your hurt, whatever painful circumstance you're dealing with, whatever promise you're waiting on, know that in Jesus, God has come near. Know that in Christ, the Holy Spirit is in you and also comes along side to be your comfort, encouragement, and strength.

And that leads to the next remarkable thing we learn about Simeon. He was uniquely attentive to the leading of the Holy Spirit. Look again at how he did life.

> . . . the **Holy Spirit** was on him. [26]It had been revealed to him by the **Holy Spirit** that he would not die before he had seen the Lord's Messiah. [27]Moved by the **Spirit**, he went into the temple courts. (Luke 2:25-27)

Three times, we see the interaction between Simeon and the Holy Spirit. The Holy Spirit was upon him – there was interaction and the working of the Holy Spirit in his life. The Holy Spirit revealed things to him – Simeon was alert and attentive. The Holy Spirit moved him – he was uniquely guided by the Holy Spirt in life.

Simeon sets a stellar example of how we as believers should be attune to the Spirit's ministry in our lives. We should be filled with or controlled by, taught by, and led by the Holy Spirit. It should be a way of life for us. It makes me question, am I, like Simeon, deeply connected with what the Holy Spirit wants to do in my life? Am I alert and responsive to His voice and leading? What role does the Holy Spirit play in your life throughout each day?

> When the parents brought in the child Jesus to do for him what the custom of the Law required, 28Simeon took him in his arms and praised God, saying:
>
> 29"Sovereign Lord, as you have promised, you may now dismiss your servant in peace. 30For my eyes have seen **your salvation**, 31which you have prepared in the sight of all nations: 32a light for **revelation to the Gentiles**, and the **glory of your people** Israel." 33The child's father and mother marveled at what was said about him. 34Then Simeon blessed them and said to Mary, his mother: "This child is destined to **cause the falling and rising** of many in Israel, and to be a sign that will be **spoken against**, 35so that the **thoughts of many hearts will be revealed. And a sword will pierce your own soul** too." (Luke 2:25-35)

Wow! Because Simeon was so attuned to the Spirit, he saw things and understood things most didn't. Salvation for the whole world, not just the Jews. The acceptance and rejection Jesus would encounter. The anguish Mary would experience at Jesus' crucifixion. Simeon saw Jesus the way no one else did.

How do you see Jesus this Christmas? Who is He . . . **to you**?

The backstory of Simeon?
Righteous. Devout. Expectant waiter.
Controlled by the Spirit. Attentive to the Spirit. Led by the Spirit.
What's my backstory this Christmas?

MAGI

Doing Right – No Matter What

Jesus was born in Bethlehem in Judea, during the reign of King Herod. About that time some wise men from eastern lands arrived in Jerusalem, asking, 2"Where is the newborn king of the Jews? We saw his star as it rose, and we have come to worship him." 3King Herod was deeply disturbed when he heard this, as was everyone in Jerusalem.

4He called a meeting of the leading priests and teachers of religious law and asked, "Where is the Messiah supposed to be born?" 5"In Bethlehem in Judea," they said, "for this is what the prophet wrote: 6'And you, O Bethlehem in the land of Judah, are not least among the ruling cities of Judah, for a ruler will come from you who will be the shepherd for my people Israel.'"

7Then Herod called for a private meeting with the wise men, and he learned from them the time when the star first appeared. 8Then he told them, "Go to Bethlehem and search carefully for the child. And when you find him, come back and tell me so that I can go and worship him, too!"

9After this interview the wise men went their way. And the star they had seen in the east guided them to Bethlehem. It went ahead of them and stopped over the place where the child was. 10When they saw the star, they were filled with joy! 11They entered the house and saw the child with his mother, Mary, and they bowed down and worshiped him. Then they opened their treasure chests and gave him gifts of gold, frankincense, and myrrh. 12When it was time to leave, they returned to their own country by another route, for God had warned them in a dream not to return to Herod. (Matthew 2:1-12)

When it comes to the backstory of the wise men, or, more precisely Magi, tradition has caused a bit of confusion. I grew up being taught there were three "**wise men**". But we also sang, "We three **kings** of Orient are . . ." But, when you look at the biblical account, it doesn't say there were three of them – whichever they were. The song included thoughts about the significance of their three gifts. Now there may be some grounds for speculating on the meaning of each gift, but again, it's not in Scripture.

And what about their identity? Do a Christmas trivia question, and some would be confident they know the names of each one. Of course, there would be three of them. And, what about the various ways of naming them? "Kings"? We'll see we can throw that out. "Wise men"? Well, we might be on to something here. "Magi"? Now we are really just using the Greek word transferred into English. But that's the best place to start to understand the backstory of who these guys were.

According to historians, magi were religious astrologers, sometimes performing priestly duties or even magic in pagan cultures. They believed they could predict history by observing the stars. Because of this, they were often called in by rulers to give them council. This gives a good explanation of why they followed the star to find Jesus.

When they arrive and announce they are looking for a king, Herod blows his stack! He calls in his own advisers and discovers that Micah had prophesied the birth of a great ruler for Israel. So Herod tells the magi to go find the baby and report back to him.

The magi follow the star to Bethlehem, present their gifts, and worship Jesus. Their mission was complete. Except one thing. They had to go back and inform Herod of what they had found. Or not.

God warned the magi not to return to Herod. So they didn't. They returned home by another route.

Simple enough, right? I don't thing so. Think about this with me. The ruler of the area had told them to report back to him. That's no small thing. These guys would know about the power and authority of a ruler like that. Bethlehem was not that far from Jerusalem. How would they know Herod did not have someone on their tail to make sure what was going on? (That's the way it always happens in the spy novels and in the movies, right?) And, add to this that Herod did find out where Jesus was born. No, it was no small thing for the magi to ignore Herod's command and sneak off.

But they made the hard choice to obey God even though it could cost them their lives. That's not being overly dramatic! Remember the babies? This guy was ruthless and had a hot temper. The magi had already seen how agitated he could get. But they chose to do the right thing.

We may never face a choice anywhere close to this in terms of the potential consequences. But we all face choices. Choices to do the right thing in obedience to God when it will cost us something.

Abraham chose to obey God and leave his home. Joseph had to choose to obey God and run away from Potiphar's wife. Moses had to choose to obey God to lead Israel rather than live large in Pharaoh's palace. Daniel had to choose to obey God even though he knew he would be thrown to the lions. Shadrach, Meshach, and Abednego had to choose obedience in the face of being thrown into a blazing furnace. The list goes on and on.

The apostles were commanded by the religious authorities to never preach in the name of Jesus. They responded, "We must obey God rather than men." (Acts 5:29)

And how can we overlook the Apostle Paul? He was called to faith in Christ. That wasn't a small step of obedience. Remember, he had been persecuting Christians. And he was not alone in that. He knew he was choosing the other side of persecution. And then he chose the step of obedience to be a preacher of the gospel. Now he was really running into the fire! Then, if that were not enough, he repeatedly faced beatings. And he continued to choose obedience. What an example for us!

There will be times in all of our lives when the choice to obey will include the expectation of it going bad for us. The boss wants you to do something unethical or even illegal. Your good friend wants you to join them in doing something you know is wrong. Being honest will cost you money. The person you're dating wants you to do something immoral. You're tempted to lie to cover up a mistake.

Remember those magi who obeyed God even though their lives were at stake? They weren't Jews. They had no allegiance to God. They surely hadn't entered into a relationship with God through Christ. And yet, they obeyed.

Sometimes those who reject God can be more obedient to God than those of us who claim to be Christ-followers.

Don't let that be true of you.

Choose obedience.

No matter what!

Christmas is the celebration of Jesus' choice to leave the glories of heaven and step down into this messed up world. He came. He lived in obedience, perfectly. Then, he chose to obey and go to the cross.

Christmas is the celebration of the One who chose to obey.
As you celebrate Jesus, choose to live like Jesus.
Choose obedience.

PART THREE:

Mary

MARY

Undeserving

Mary. What do we do with her? Some pay little attention to her, while others come close to treating her as equal to Jesus. Neither are appropriate. It is clear that Mary provides a great model for us in many ways that we will explore. But Mary was just a normal, sinful human being. She needed that Savior she would give birth to, just like all of us.

So why did God choose Mary to be the mother of Jesus? She certainly was a godly young lady who quickly surrendered to God's plan for her life. Is that why God choose her? Was it actually some merit, some goodness God saw in her that prompted Him to choose her?

God does look for faithful and surrendered people to use at times. But there are certainly other times where people were intent on sin and running away from God and God captured their hearts and turned them around to pursue Him. Saul/Paul is one example. I am another.

Scripture clearly teaches that all of us are bent toward sin and rebellion against God. We are not all equal in the extent of our rebellion against God before accepting Christ as Savior, but we all were rebellious on some level.

> Once you were alienated from God and were enemies in your minds because of your evil behavior. (Colossians 1:21)

So, where does that leave us in the whole backstory of Mary? It leaves us at the place of recognizing one foundational truth. Mary was not chosen by God because she deserved it. God could have found, or even raised up another young lady to be the mother of Jesus. We know God had a choice. It wasn't because God had to choose Mary. And perhaps it's in these truths that we capture the true backstory of Mary becoming the mother of Jesus. God chose her, not because of who she was, but simply as an act of His sovereign choice, mercy, and grace. See if you don't pick up on this backstory as you read the account of the angel visiting Mary.

> Gabriel appeared to her and said, "Greetings, favored woman! The Lord is with you!" 29Confused and disturbed, Mary tried to think what the angel could mean. 30"Don't be afraid, Mary," the angel told her, "for you have found favor with God! (Luke 1:28-30)

Gabriel calls Mary a "favored woman." Literally translated, this means, "to be given grace." It isn't that Mary possessed grace – a quality of elegance, refinement or charm, some internal goodness. No, Mary is given grace – God's free gift of some blessing to the undeserving. We know this is the case, because Gabriel also says, "you have found favor (grace) with God"

Grace. That's it. Pure and simple. But so profound and glorious.

Grace.

That's what moved God to choose Mary. And Mary understood this. Mary wasn't expecting this. She had no thought that she had some elevated status with God. She knew what this was all about – exalting God's glory. She knew her position before God – God's servant.

> And Mary said: "My soul **glorifies the Lord** 47and my spirit rejoices in God **my Savior**, 48for he has been mindful of the **humble state of his servant**. From now on all generations will call me blessed, 49for the Mighty One has done great things for me-- holy is his name. 50His **mercy** extends to those who fear him, from generation to generation. 51He has performed mighty deeds with his arm; he has scattered those who are proud in their inmost thoughts. 52He has brought down rulers from their thrones but has lifted up the humble. 53He has filled the hungry with good things but has sent the rich away empty. 54He has helped his servant Israel, remembering to be merciful 55to Abraham and his descendants forever, just as he promised our ancestors." (Luke 1:46-55)

Do you see her focus? Do you see her view of herself? Do you her view of her need? It's all about God. Her focus is on praising and worshiping God for what **He** has done. She is a recipient of grace and mercy – a Savior!

It is interesting to note that after Mary praises God for His present blessing and gift of grace to her, she looks back. She speaks of God's relationship with Israel. And she sees all of what is happening fitting in with God's mercy and grace toward Israel and His promises to Israel. And so, we must dig deeper into the backstory.

Israel. God's chosen people. Recipients of God's mercy and grace over and over again. That's their story. Israel kept running into rebellion, unfaithfulness, and sin. God continually brought them back to Himself. God. In Psalm 106, David puts this backstory on full display. A few verses summarize the message.

> 6Like our ancestors, we have sinned. We have done wrong! We have acted wickedly! . . . 44Even so, he pitied them in their distress and listened to their cries. 45He remembered his covenant with them and relented because of his unfailing love. (Psalm 106:6, 44-45)

This is the story of Israel: God's continuing faithfulness in spite of Israel's repetitive unfaithfulness. In fact, Israel's unfaithfulness was so bad that at one point He compared them to a wild donkey in heat (Jeremiah 2:24).

So why didn't He give up on them? Why not destroy them for their unfaithfulness? Mary pointed to God's mercy and promises as the answer. David points to God's covenant and unfailing love.

This "unfailing love" is rooted in the Hebrew word, "chesed." It is translated lovingkindness, faithful love, loyal love. It is an incredibly rich word speaking of God's loyal, covenant or promised love. Some have called it the most important word in the Old Testament. In this word, God's love and actions are uniquely intertwined as it shows God's covenant love producing generous acts of kindness. And we see God's lovingkindness displayed *in spite of*, rather than **because of** the obedience of the people. In the New Testament, it is expressed in the ideas of grace, mercy, and love, all of which are given to the believer in Christ.

This is the true backstory of Mary being selected to be the mother of Jesus – God's gracious love and mercy. The truth is that God chooses and uses, and richly blesses us – the undeserving. This is the true backstory of Jesus coming. It is the amazing reality of our celebration of Jesus' birth. He came, not because we deserved it, but in spite of the fact that we could never deserve Him, or His blessing.

God blesses even when we are living very carnally. The fact that one can be healthy while living in rebellion against God is a clear example of God's kindness in spite of our behavior.

> And Mary said: "My soul **glorifies the Lord** [47]and my spirit rejoices in God **my Savior**, [48]for he has been mindful of the **humble state of his servant**. (Luke 1:47-48)

Mary got that she didn't deserve God's blessing. Do **you** get it?

We should be deeply humbled by the glory of Christmas. Jesus came to this earth to be born in a cattle stall. He came to die for sinners like you and me. What grace. What mercy. What **underserved** love!

This Christmas, may our hearts join with the heart of Mary and declare, "I glorify and praise you God, my Savior. Thank you for your gift of grace, mercy, & love – to me, the undeserving."

MARY

Unexpected

God sent the angel Gabriel to Nazareth, a village in Galilee, ²⁷to a virgin named Mary. She was engaged to be married to a man named Joseph, a descendant of King David. ²⁸Gabriel appeared to her and said, "Greetings, favored woman! The Lord is with you!" ²⁹Confused and disturbed, Mary tried to think what the angel could mean. ³⁰"Don't be afraid, Mary," the angel told her, "for you have found favor with God! ³¹You will conceive and give birth to a son, and you will name him Jesus. ³²He will be very great and will be called the Son of the Most High. The Lord God will give him the throne of his ancestor David. ³³And he will reign over Israel forever; his Kingdom will never end!" ³⁴Mary asked the angel, "But how can this happen? I am a virgin." ³⁵The angel replied, "The Holy Spirit will come upon you, and the power of the Most High will overshadow you. So the baby to be born will be holy, and he will be called the Son of God. (Luke 1:26-35)

SURPRISE! You're going to have a baby! Um, what? That would be shocking and unexpected even under more normal circumstances. But Mary wasn't married. She wasn't sexually active. And she never had been! Didn't see that coming.

Seriously, try to put yourself in Mary's position. First, an angel shows up in front of you. Afraid? Duh! And then the angel jumps right into some mind-blowing statements. The angel didn't give it to her slowly, like, "Mary, I have some things to tell you that are going to be hard to understand and accept, so bear with me, just listen to the whole story." No, this angel pretty much just got to the point. "You're gonna have a baby. The Son of God. And He will rule over Israel. Forever."

Shock. Confusion. Questions. "How can this happen, I'm a virgin." "Oh, no problem, "The Holy Spirit will come upon you, and the power of the Most High will overshadow you." What does that mean?!?

Maybe you guys aren't there, but you ladies are. That sounds extremely intimidating! Please understand, I don't want to be inappropriate with this, but Mary had to be pretty overwhelmed by this idea.

This is seriously big, way-out-in-left-field, unexpected stuff. This is scary. This is the kind of invitation where you send regrets. Look, we know the whole story, but if you didn't know, how would you have responded if you were Mary? This is some seriously heavy backstory to think about!

What if God throws a curve ball like this in your direction? Disease. Cancer. Significant career or job upheaval. Financial crisis. A relationship breakdown out of nowhere. God calls you to do something unusual, beyond you.

Listen, this isn't an unusual thing for God. He regularly calls people to things that just don't make much sense.

What if God wanted to do something God-sized in your life? Would you just dismiss it? The issue actually isn't just our view of the impossible. Our view of God will have a significant impact on how we see and respond to the impossible.

Think about this carefully. If I am only willing to think in terms of what I am able to do or what others can help me do, I won't even be able to think about the great things God can do. When God tries to lead me in a direction or lead me to do something, and I can't figure out how I could do it, I will simply say it's not possible. The task looks too big to me. The opposition will be too great. I don't have the resources. You see where the focus is? It is on me and my abilities, not on God and His ability. God could be trying to tell me to move forward and do something, but my excuses, based on my focus on me and my inability, will block my hearing!

On the other hand, people who realize they serve a God of limitless power will be able to see the big things God wants to do through them. Yes, they will see their inability and not deny it. But they will choose to focus on God's ability and obey God's lead by faith.

Are you familiar with the story of Gideon in the Old Testament? Let me take you back there. God commands Gideon to lead an army to war, but Gideon isn't even a seasoned military commander. And, the enemy has Gideon outnumbered 4 to 1! But then, God tells Gideon he has too many men and he needs to send some of them home. After this cut, Gideon is outnumbered 13 to 1! So, each of Gideon's soldiers will have to fight against 13 enemy soldiers!

God's not done yet. He tells Gideon there are still too many soldiers in his army. He says He wants to make sure that when it's all over it is perfectly clear that He is the one who brought the victory.

There's another cut. Now, each of Gideon's soldiers will have to fight 450 enemy soldiers! Would any military strategist consider this a good plan? Would anyone expect to have a remote chance of winning under this plan? Well, maybe if they have vastly superior weapons. No, no weapons. None. Just horns and flashlights (trumpets and lamps). But the enemy army is defeated – wiped out, really – by the power of God!

This is just one of many stories we can tell from Scripture where, from a human perspective, what God called his people to do was either impossible or ridiculous. Here's a list of a few in Scripture:

Noah – build a boat because there's going to be a flood. A what?
Abraham – leave your home. I'll show you later where you're going.
Abraham – kill the son I promised you would be your heir.
Moses – go back to Egypt where you're a wanted man.
Moses – part the Red Sea with your rod.
Joshua – march around the enemy city.
Gideon – get rid of your army and go to war with lamps and horns.
Isaiah – walk around barefoot and naked. (Isaiah 20)
Jeremiah – buy underwear, wear it, then hide it by the river. (Jer. 13)
Ezekiel – attack a clay model of Jerusalem. (Ezekiel 4)

Hosea – marry a prostitute who won't quit. (Hosea 1)

In these situations, God led His people to do things that were laughable from a human perspective. But God's people focused on a powerful God. They knew God had commanded. They believed God was able. They stepped forward by faith.

When it comes to stepping into the impossible, there is a critical first step. God must give the call. It must be God's will. We don't devise our own plans for what we are going to do and then go to God to get His approval and provision. No, we seek His leading, we trust Him, even for things that are bigger than us and our resources, and we step out in faith. Hearing direction from God and knowing His will must come first. God directs us to do extraordinary things He has planned, and we must accept the assignment rather than dismiss it as illogical.

So now I ask you. Will you be like Mary and follow God into something, even though you don't know how it can work? Can God lead you to do something bigger than yourself? Is there something God has been trying to lead you to do that you have dismissed because you can't see how it is possible?

The angel's final words to Mary?

"For nothing is impossible with God." (Luke 1:37)

Do you truly believe that?

MARY
Unprepared

God sent the angel Gabriel to Nazareth, a village in Galilee, ²⁷to a virgin named Mary. (Luke 1:26-27)

Unprepared. That's an understatement. We don't have a prolonged biography of Mary in Scripture, but it is clear that, on many levels, she wasn't prepared for this. This is the backstory.

The first glaring indication that Mary would not be ready for this is her age and stage of life. She was an engaged virgin. Bible scholars agree that this would make her about 14 years old. A teenager. Sure, things were a bit different in that culture and she would have been better prepared than most teens in western cultures today. Still, she was just barely getting started in life. She didn't have a few years of experience as a woman, or as a mother. She didn't have experience in much at all, really. And then, there is the issue of where she grew up.

> Nazareth was a lovely little town snuggled in the hills overlooking the broad and fertile Plain of Esdraelon. It consisted primarily of some small white stone houses, a synagogue built on its highest knoll, and a marketplace at the entrance to the village. When the New Testament era dawned, its population seems to have numbered little more than one hundred, mostly farmers, but also some skilled craftsmen whose shops were found in the marketplace—a potter, a weaver, a dyer, a blacksmith, and a carpenter. (Richard L. Strauss)

Yeah, not an up-and-coming village. No impressive, well-rounded education. No connections with movers and shakers. No connections at all, for that matter. What did Mary have to prepare her to raise a child at this point in her life? And, not just any child. The Son of God!

Unprepared. Unqualified. Too young. Not enough experience. Again, this isn't just a Christmas backstory thing. Once more, if we trace our way through the Scriptures, we find more examples of young and unprepared people God used. There are several important young people in the history of Israel that were most likely in their teens or very early 20s when used by God. Miriam, Joseph, David, Daniel, Shadrach, Meshach, Abednego, Jeremiah, Esther, Ruth. And then there were two godly kings who hadn't reached 10 years old, Josiah and Joash.

People may not respect the young or inexperienced. They might not give them a chance. But God does.

I have often heard people refer to the youth in a church as "the church of tomorrow." Nonsense! That is so offensive and just wrong. If a teen is a genuine Christ-follower, they are the church of today. And the reality is that many times our teens are more faithful, do more in ministry, and are more mature spiritually than the adults. Who keeps the children's ministries going? In many churches, it's the teens. Who goes on the missions trips? Many times, it's the teens. Who is more likely to respond appropriately to worship styles they don't prefer? The teens, hands down.

Can we do something this Christmas and beyond? Can we honor the reality that God chose a young lady – a teen – to be the mother of Jesus? Can we start giving our teens who are following Christ the respect they deserve?

Age and experience are not qualifications God demands in order to use us for His purposes. You don't need a great education or seminary degree to make a difference for Jesus Christ. Mary was a simple country girl.

Think about Jesus' disciples. Were they really prepared when Jesus launched them off to change the world after He returned to heaven? Absolutely not! They were just ordinary guys. Working men. And everyone knew they didn't have the training or qualifications.

When they saw the courage of Peter and John and realized that they were unschooled, ordinary men, they were astonished and they took note that these men had been with Jesus. (Acts 4:13)

Unschooled. Ordinary. Fishermen. Astonishing! What was their great preparation to turn the world upside down? What prepared them to stand before thousands and share the gospel, with thousands accepting Christ?

They had been with Jesus. That's what prepared them. Sure, they had learned much from Jesus. But they had no formal training in theology. No speech classes. No instruction on how to put together a compelling 3-point sermon. No class on how to craft a message. There were no seminars on vision casting, strategic planning, or multi-site ministry. And the only "branding" they understood was Jesus.

Look, the point isn't that these things have no place in the church or ministry, but when these things become the major focus, we're missing something. Preparation and organization do matter, but the consistent examples of Scripture emphasize God's part in effective ministry, not ours. We need to be careful that we don't value these things above the leading and empowering of the Holy Spirit.

 And that leads us back to the example of the disciples. The religious leaders were astonished because they didn't have all the right education and accomplishments on their resumes. Instead, their resumes were packed with just one key essential: they had spent time with Jesus.

This is the key for all of us in life, and in ministry. The breadth of our impact will be inseparably linked to the depth of our relationship with God. Jesus used an amazing illustration to help us understand how people who are unprepared in the world's eyes – people like Mary and the disciples – are prepared and empowered to make a difference.

Remain in me, and I will remain in you. For a branch cannot produce fruit if it is severed from the vine, and you cannot be fruitful unless you remain in me. 5"Yes, I am the vine; you are the branches. Those who remain in me, and I in them, will produce much fruit. For apart from me you can do nothing. (John 15:4-5)

This illustration pictures the most vital preparation for life. We get prepared by cultivating intimacy with Christ. His life-giving, ministry-empowering presence in our lives is what prepares and qualifies us for what He leads us to do.

"When you are brought before synagogues, rulers and authorities, do not worry about how you will defend yourselves or what you will say, ¹²for the Holy Spirit will teach you at that time what you should say." (Luke 12:11)

I like that. Preparation is important. Winging it is not a plan. But the critical element to preparation is staying connected to Jesus. And in the times when God leads me into something intimidating that I feel unprepared for, I can be confident that the Holy Spirit will be there to guide me.

Unprepared? Unschooled? Unqualified? Inexperienced?

Not a problem.

God can and will use you!

Just like Mary.

Prepare by staying connected to Jesus.

Be sensitive and responsive to the ministry of the Holy Spirit.

If God has called you to it, He will lead you through it.

MARY

Unscripted

God sent the angel Gabriel to Nazareth, a village in Galilee, ²⁷to
a virgin named Mary. She was engaged to be married to a man
named Joseph, a descendant of King David. ²⁸Gabriel appeared
to her and said, "Greetings, favored woman! The Lord is with
you!" ²⁹Confused and disturbed, Mary tried to think what the
angel could mean. ³⁰"Don't be afraid, Mary," the angel told her,
"for you have found favor with God! ³¹You will conceive and
give birth to a son, and you will name him Jesus. (Luke 1:26-31)

This was not the way Mary planned to get her life started with Joseph. A
baby does indeed change everything. They probably wouldn't have
waited too long to start a family given the cultural priority to have
children. But not like this. This wasn't the script. This is not the
backstory Mary envisioned for her life.

All of us have a script we've written for our lives. We like to think that
our lives are ours to live as we want. We have our ideas, we make our
plans, and we set out to fulfill our plans. Make plans. Set goals. Position
yourself. Determine your destiny. That's how you do life to get the most
out of it you can. We don't like other people telling us what to do and
how to live our lives. We don't like it when someone or something
frustrates our plans for our lives.

Even God.

But that's exactly what He does.

> We can make our plans, but the LORD determines our steps.
> (Proverbs 16:9)

We may throw the dice, but the LORD determines how they fall. (Proverbs 16:33)

A man's steps are determined by the LORD, so how can anyone understand his own way? (Proverbs 20:24)

Who has spoken and it came to pass, unless the Lord has commanded it? (Lamentations 3:37)

These verses may catch you off guard if you have not read them before. They just don't fit with our perception of life. We think everything rises and falls on our choices and actions. We think we write the script of our lives. We decide what to do and just do it, and that's that. We know what we know. We make choices, and our choices lead to actions and results. That's how life works – so we think. But what we miss is how God is behind the scenes orchestrating the whole script without forcing us to do anything. And sometimes, we get so focused on the script we have written for our lives that God's script for us totally spins us around.

The first step to accepting the unscripted is for me to make a complete surrender of my life to God. I must surrender my plans and goals and live my life with an earnest passion to know and live out God's plans and goals for my life. This is the only way of living that leads to a truly meaningful life, an invested life. When I live my way, by my plans, for my goals, I end up with a short-sighted and largely wasted life.

If you try to hang on to your life, you will lose it. But if you give up your life for my sake, you will save it. (Matthew 16:25)

Here's what I get from what Jesus is saying here. If I am determined to pursue my script for my life, I will actually be writing a script that leads me to missing out on the best life for me. But if I seek His guidance and I follow His script, I will experience life to the fullest.

But sometimes, it's just really hard for us to accept this truth. We honestly think we have a great, well thought out plan. We've figured it out and know where we're headed and the best way to get there....or so we think!

There is a way that seems right to a man, but its end is the way to death. (Proverbs 14:12 ESV)

This verse states very plainly that it is foolish to trust in and rely on even our best ideas. They may seem like great ideas, thoughts, and plans. We think we're really smart and wise. But in the end, it leads to foolishness and even death.

If we're honest, most of us have probably been at a place in life at one time or another when we were hanging on and unwilling to let go. Maybe a financial goal. An inappropriate relationship. A career goal. You fill in the blank. When we refuse to let go and allow God to write the script, what happens? Until the Apostle Paul surrendered his life to God's plan, he was fighting hard for his way. It was a futile battle. Jesus confronted him.

'Saul, Saul, why do you persecute me? It is hard for you to kick against the goads.' (Acts 26:14)

Unless you're familiar with herding cattle, this might not make sense to you. A goad is a stick with a sharp point on the end. It's also known as a cattle prod. If an ox refuses to go where the herder wants, the goad is used to make it move. Pain produces the correct response.

If we resist it when God wants to change the script, we force Him to get out the goad. There will be painful consequences. It's hard to push back against the goads. God will not give up. You're fighting a loosing battle when you fight against God.

Living out God's script for my life means I will give my life to God to use as He chooses for the purposes of His agenda, His kingdom, and for eternity. My humanly conceived script will be limited in perspective and will only impact time. God's purposes and plans are eternal. God wants me to give up my short-sighted plans to engage in activities that contribute to fulfilling His eternal purposes and plans.

Now here's the thing. Sometimes I don't want to let go of my dreams and plans. I have it all figured out. My dreams might even be focused on serving God in a certain way, in a certain place. And so, I believe I am following God's script for my life. At least I'm doing my best to follow God's script.

Then God goes off script. I'm devastated. I thought God had led me to this place. I thought I knew where God was leading me. And it was a good place. A place where I would be serving God and making a difference for Him. And God turns the page. It's nothing like I expected. How can I possibly make sense of that?

> The LORD says, "I will guide you along the best pathway for your life. I will advise you and watch over you. (Psalm 32:8)

When life goes off script, I can have peace, confidence, and hope because God is in control and He is guiding the script of my life "along the best pathway."

What if Mary pushed back against a life that was unscripted?

Is there something unscripted in your life you need to accept?

Do you need to let go of your script to surrender to God's in some area of your life?

Remember, when God goes "off script" it is *always* for our best!

**God's perfect knowledge and wisdom
produce a perfect plan for our lives
to fulfill a perfect purpose in our lives.**

MARY

Uncomfortable

Mary was living a pretty nice quiet and comfortable life in her little village of Nazareth. She was engaged to be married and must have been quite happy. Then things got a little crazy.

When you look at Mary's story and also dig deeper into the backstory, there are so many things going on to make Mary quite uncomfortable. Certainly, the initial moments of her encounter with the angel made her uncomfortable. Then there was the issue of telling Joseph about it. What tension there must have been until Joseph had his dream and was reassured that Mary was telling the truth.

Still, Mary would have the very uncomfortable task of facing family, friends, and the community. They didn't have any dreams. Could this have prompted Mary to go to Elizabeth? We don't know, but it's a good possibility.

Then there was the whole census thing. Stress. Traveling to Bethlehem had to be very uncomfortable. It was no easy journey. And then, when they arrived, they had to stay among the animals! Could it get any worse? Yes. She had to give birth right there with the animals.

Have you ever found yourself in an unfamiliar and uncomfortable situation? It can be very disorienting. You can have a hard time trying to get your bearings.

We all handle little stuff that makes us uncomfortable all the time. But when these life-altering events hit us, uncomfortable doesn't even feel like an adequate word to use. No, it's not just uncomfortable, it hurts very deeply.

So, what's God up to at these times in our lives? Is there something positive that can come out of it? It certainly can be difficult to see how it can. But Scripture actually gives us some pretty clear answers for why these painful circumstances invade our comfort. Let me share with you 7 reasons why bad things happen to good people:

❶ Bad things lead me to value a great God. They help free me from empty living and create in me a passion for God.

> O God, you are my God; I earnestly search for you. My soul thirsts for you; my whole body longs for you in this parched and weary land where there is no water. (Psalm 63:1)

> Why this intense longing and passion for God? A season of suffering. When do you pray the most? During seasons of suffering. Hard times in life help us realize what really matters in life they give us greater passion for God and that's a good thing... a very good thing!

❷ Bad things remind us that this is not our home and give us a deeper longing for heaven.

> For this world is not our permanent home; we are looking forward to a home yet to come. (Hebrews 13:14)

> This place is just a cheap, temporary rental. Hard times show us that this world is not our home and motivates us to focus on what really matters – eternity.

❸ Bad things are part of God's loving, purposeful plan to make me more like Christ.

> 6For the LORD disciplines those he loves, and he punishes each one he accepts as his child." . . . 11Now all discipline seems painful at the time, not joyful. But later it produces the fruit of peace and righteousness for those trained by it. (Hebrews 12:6,11)

We need to understand that discipline is an act of love. And discipline is not just for doing wrong, it's also to teach. Like a coach and athletic training. You might run laps as a punishment for messing around, or run laps just to improve your strength and endurance.

❹ Bad things are designed by God to strengthen our faith.

These trials will show that your faith is genuine. It is being tested as fire tests and purifies gold-- though your faith is far more precious than mere gold. So when your faith remains strong through many trials, it will bring you much praise and glory and honor on the day when Jesus Christ is revealed to the whole world. (1 Peter 1:7)

I can handle a lot more bad stuff now without falling apart than I could when I was young in my faith. As I see God care for me and lead me through painful circumstances, I grow in my faith and trust in Him. I get stronger in my faith.

❺ Bad things move us toward 100% reliance on God.

We think you ought to know, dear brothers and sisters, about the trouble we went through in the province of Asia. We were crushed and overwhelmed beyond our ability to endure, and we thought we would never live through it. ⁹In fact, we expected to die. But as a result, we stopped relying on ourselves and learned to rely only on God, who raises the dead. (2 Cor. 1:8-9)

Our first reaction to the ordinary struggles of life is to depend our ourselves. We look at the problem. We try to understand it. We evaluate our resources. We think about how to solve it. We set out on the course of action we think is best to solve the problem. Where's God in that? We don't even acknowledge His existence.

Until we face something that is so huge that we can't think about handling it on our own, we will continue to depend on our own thinking and solutions. We **need** big problems to teach us that we need to depend on a big God in everything.

❻ Bad things lead me to better love. They equip us so we can help others who face hard times.

> All praise to God, the Father of our Lord Jesus Christ. God is our merciful Father and the source of all comfort. He comforts us in all our troubles so that we can comfort others. When they are troubled, we will be able to give them the same comfort God has given us. (2 Corinthians 1:3-4)

When someone you love is hurting deeply, you really want to help, don't you? Sometimes, we don't know what to say, right? Why? Because we don't understand what they're going through. We wish we could understand, but we've never experienced what they're going through, so we can't fully understand. But if I have experienced what they are going through, then I can understand, and I can speak more compassionately. I am better equipped to help them.

❼ Bad things are a showcase for a glorious God. They demonstrate the glory of God *in* us and **THROUGH** us.

> But even if you suffer for doing what is right, God will reward you for it. So don't worry or be afraid of their threats. Instead, you must worship Christ as Lord of your life. And if someone asks about your Christian hope, always be ready to explain it. (1 Peter 3:14-15)

In the perfect wisdom of God's design:
Bad things happen to good people
to make them great people.

MARY

Uncertain

You will conceive and give birth to a son, and you will name him Jesus. ³²He will be very great and will be called the Son of the Most High. The Lord God will give him the throne of his ancestor David. ³³And he will reign over Israel forever; his Kingdom will never end!" ³⁴Mary asked the angel, "But how can this happen? I am a virgin." ³⁵The angel replied, "The Holy Spirit will come upon you, and the power of the Most High will overshadow you. So the baby to be born will be holy, and he will be called the Son of God. (Luke 1:31-35)

Have you ever wondered how much Mary understood of what the angel said? Sure, she understood some, maybe quite a bit – she did seem to have a good grasp of Old Testament prophecies. But still, that was mostly broad brush strokes. She could understand the basic idea that she would have a baby while remaining a virgin. But as we've touched on before, what does that mean? The concept of giving birth to the Son of God is understandable – at least the words are clear enough. But what was really going to take place? I mean really, if I'm Mary I want some clearer explanation of the details.

Of course, there wouldn't have just been uncertainty surrounding how she would actually become pregnant and all the questions about carrying the Son of God in her womb. There was so much more! How would Joseph respond? And what about her family, her community? What will life be like as Jesus grows up? And what about the future for her Son?

For Mary, this would be very uncomfortable as we have discovered. But, there's another aspect of this. The unknown, or "what-ifs" could consume you in a situation like this. Knowing that God is in this and is working out His plan is great. But our restless souls that fight to be in the know, and even in control, push back against being in the dark. "God, I'm thankful that you are God and you have all this under control. I know you are working out your good plan in my life. But can you just show me where we're headed?"

Uncertainty is focused on a future we don't know about. When this uncertainty involves issues we care about and things that could go south, it produces fear and anxiety.

If I don't know if I will find a job, the uncertainty causes fear. If I don't know how I will pay my bills, the uncertainty causes anxiety. When I'm not sure if the doctors will find a cure, this uncertainty tears at me. When I don't know if my relationship can be saved, the uncertainty leads to emotional distress. I don't like the unknown. Right?

When we face any kind of uncertainty, we begin to come up with all kinds of questions and our minds can run into some very dark places. The "what-ifs" fill our thoughts.

But what if the "what-ifs" don't matter?

When our uncertainties lead us to anxiety, fear, and despair, we often work feverishly to find answers and solutions. We plot the way forward. We try to predict, plan, and produce the future we want. Again, the "what-ifs" creep in. "What if I can . . . ." "What if they . . . then I will be able to . . ." "What if the doctor is wrong about . . ."

Again, what if the what-ifs don't matter?

You see, when we don't know the path forward, life can really get quite stressful, right? This jumble of doubts, fears, anxiety, and "what-ifs" can consume us. We cry out to God and want Him to give us all the answers and certainty we want regarding our future. And we can get very impatient. "God, I promise I'll follow your lead. So can you just go ahead and lead? Show me where we're going? I'm ready, it's time!"

When someone arrives late or finishes something much later than we expected we will often use the word "finally." "You're *finally* here!" "You *finally* got that done?" "You *finally* have the answers I've been waiting for." We imply that their timing was off a bit. If we are bolder, we might even tell them that they should have arrived, accomplished the task, or had the answers sooner.

There is never a "finally" with God. Never! The fact that God is above time and controls time means that God has perfect timing all the time. It also means that God will never be too fast or too slow in what He does. It means that nothing can hinder the perfect execution of God's perfect plan at the perfect time. God will always have perfect timing in clearing the fog of uncertainty in our lives.

God always has perfect timing. Our big challenge is that we need to wait on God's timing – even when it leaves us in a place of uncertainty in the present. When we don't know what's happening or where we're headed, we quickly become agitated if we don't maintain this critical perspective.

Don't get impatient and believe the lie that you have to make a decision. If God has not given you direction, wait. "But the sale will be over!" "But the deal will be lost!" "But I will miss this opportunity!" If God doesn't give the go ahead to move forward, stay put! If God hasn't given you the answer yet, He has a very good reason. Wait.

Are you frustrated, waiting on God to speak or act? Be still and listen. Contemplate the truth that there is a God in heaven who in in absolute control, and who has perfect timing, every time. Wait for His leading out of the uncertainties. He is working, and He will bring you through this. Wait for His direction. His way is the best way – by far. Let Him lead you. Follow Him patiently, one step at a time. Don't hesitate when He shows you a step to take. Don't move when He wants you to stay put. And don't delay when He tells you to move.

What if the "what-ifs" DON'T matter?

You don't need to be afraid or anxious about the future. God has given you way too many promises for you to question what He is doing in your life and what He has in store for you.

What if the "what-ifs" don't matter because God is sovereign over your "what-ifs"?

He is!

"But my future is so full of uncertainties! In fact, there's hardly anything I am certain of." Here is a critical truth:

In the face of uncertainty,
the only certainties that matter are that
God knows!
God has a plan!
God is in control!
I can trust Him with my life!

Do you remember how Mary responded to all her uncertainty?

"I am the Lord's slave,
may it be done to me according to your word." (Luke 1:38)

Don't miss her perspective and commitment. It is powerful. She saw herself as God's *slave*. Rights? Surrendered. Willingly. Any say in how her life would go? Surrendered. Willingly. Any questioning the plan or pushing back? Surrendered. Willingly. Any demand to have the uncertainties cleared up? Surrendered. Willingly.

Oh, that we would be like Mary this Christmas. Surrendered to the will and plan of God. Even if that surrender includes embracing uncertainty.

Will you join Mary and make this declaration this Christmas?

"Lord, I am Your slave,
may it be done to me according to your word – I'm surrendered."

PART FOUR:

Jesus

DECEMBER 24TH

JESUS

The Eternal Word

It's Christmas eve. Tomorrow, we celebrate Jesus' birth – His entry into this world. In our devotional journey so far, we have focused on the backstories of Christmas traditions. We've thought about the backstories of people who played a part in the story of Jesus birth, and have highlighted Mary's backstory for the last several days.

But today, as we anticipate celebrating the birth of Jesus, perhaps it is fitting to consider the backstory of Jesus. What's the story behind the story of the day Jesus was born in Bethlehem? So today, we will explore the day before – and more.

When we go to the gospels to discover Jesus' story. Mark takes us back to the beginning of Jesus' ministry. Matthew and Luke take us back a bit further, to the beginning of Jesus' life – to His birth. But when we look at the gospel of John, he takes us back even further – to the beginning, and even before the beginning. The amazing, wonderful backstory of Jesus **before** His birth.

> In the beginning was the Word, and the Word was with God, and the Word was God. [2]He was in the beginning with God. [3]All things were made through him, and without him was not any thing made that was made. (John 1:1-3)

> [14]And the Word became flesh, and dwelt among us, and we saw His glory, glory as of the only begotten from the Father, full of grace and truth. (John 1:14)

As John tells us the story of Jesus, he introduces us to the eternal "Word", made flesh. Since John is writing to Greeks, he uses their own philosophical term *logos* (translated, "word") as the starting point for his message.

The Greek thinking behind this *logos*/word is somewhat complex. It was, for them, much more than just a word, *logos*. It was an idea. More appropriately, it was a set of ideas. Bear with me as this gets a little deep for a moment.

As a Greek philosophical term, *logos* was the soul of the universe. They observed order in the universe and believed there must be some rational force behind that order. It only makes sense. Order must have something that created it.

For the Greeks, this was an **impersonal** force and was a part of everything and governed everything. It was believed to be the creative force for everything and the source of wisdom for humanity.

When John uses the Greek idea of *logos*, he makes it **personal**. He says there is a real, living, personal God who is involved in life. The *logos* stepped into the world of humanity as a living, breathing person. The baby in a manger. Rather than an impersonal and uninvolved force, John presents a person who loves, cares, has compassion, and comes to the aid of people in a personal relationship.

So, John presents Jesus, not just as the true *logos* (word), but as much more. The *logos* was in the beginning. Really, **before** the beginning – all things were created by Him and nothing exists that was not created by Him.

Jesus had an existence before His birth at Bethlehem. He existed before angels and archangels, who are created beings. He "was" – therefore, He was uncreated. There never was a time when Christ was not.

"With God" asserts the distinct personality of the Son in the Godhead. Jesus is not an impersonal "force" as the Greeks thought. He is a real person, able to relate personally to us.

John clearly states, "The Word was God". That statement, "was God" places Jesus – the Word – within the unity of the Godhead in oneness with the Father. Jesus, the Son of God, is eternally God the Son— 100% God with all His nature and character.

The Word "became flesh and dwelt among us" (v. 14). The word defines God in general concepts and ideas to give us the "big picture" of who God is. Paul puts it this way:

> God, after He spoke long ago to the fathers in the prophets in many portions and in many ways, [2]in these last days has **spoken to us in His Son**, whom He appointed heir of all things, through whom also He made the world. (Hebrews 1:1-2)

Jesus Christ is the Word. As such He is the essential revealer of the divine triune God. As the *logos*, Jesus is the one through whom God expressed Himself. Jesus, the living Word, unveiled God's hidden glory. In Him the Father becomes known, because God has "in these last days spoken fully and completely in His Son."

Jesus demonstrates the greatness and glory of God in all its magnificent brilliance. Jesus helps us understand how the character of God acts in practical ways in the physical, human world.

You cannot fully know God if you don't fully know Christ!

If you want to know about God – Look at Jesus!
What does God value? – Look at Jesus!
How does God think? – Look at Jesus!
What does God do? – Look at Jesus!
How does God focus His time? – Look at Jesus!
How does God invest His resources? – Look at Jesus!

If you want to know what the glory of God looks like, if you want to see what a glorious life looks like, look at Jesus!

So what can we take away from this somewhat deep look at the backstory of Jesus? Here are few very practical things for us to think about and act on.

1. Jesus gave up the glories of His eternal existence in Heaven with the Father *for us*. What will you sacrifice this Christmas for Him? To serve others?

2. The eternal Son of God clothed Himself with humanity. Are you willing to get in the dirt – to inconvenience yourself – to show God's love to someone?

3. God is so passionate about a relationship with us that He took on humanity. How passionate are you about your relationship with Him?

4. The incarnation clearly communicates how much God loves us. How are you doing at communicating His love to others?

5. Jesus took on human form, honoring God in that body. How are you doing at honoring God in your "human form"?

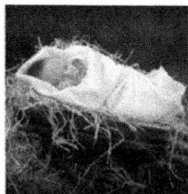

JESUS

Immanuel – God with us!

MERRY CHRISTMAS!

Welcome to the wonder and majesty of Jesus' birth!

The wonder of what we celebrate today is normally the stuff of fiction. You can read about it in fairy tales and novels. You can see it in cartoons and movies. But it just doesn't happen in real life.

Jasmine was drawn outside the palace walls to befriend a peasant boy. She dressed like Aladdin and mingled with the people in the market. She even got herself in trouble with the palace guard along with Aladdin. But that was simply Disney's fantasy. This just doesn't happen in real life. Princesses don't do these kinds of things.

Mischief and mayhem followed when Young Prince Edward switched places with pauper Tom Canty in Mark Twain's novel-made-movie *The Prince and the Pauper*. But this just doesn't happen in real life. Princes don't switch places with paupers.

Princesses and princes, kings and queens, presidents, and celebrities. They all have something in common. They tend to stay away from, and even remain isolated and protected from us common folk. Oh, they'll make occasional, brief appearances and even mingle a bit with us, but we know they aren't eager to identify with us. We know they aren't looking to be our friends or build a relationship with us. No, they're elite. We're just ordinary people. And they're happy to keep it that way, thank you very much.

But every once in a while, someone special comes along. They're one of the elite, but they don't act like it. They actually **do** want to intermingle.

They actually **do** build relationships with the ordinary people. And they stand out. People take notice. They are unique, special.

Princess Diana was that kind of person. She was so approachable that she was called "the people's princess." She gave everyone the feeling they could be her friend. She didn't act like she was different or above others. She really did step out of the palace and intermingle with the common folk. In fact, in 1987 she was one of the first high-profile celebrities to be photographed touching one of the most "untouchables" of society at the time, a person infected with HIV. She was greatly admired. When she died, it was not just the people of England who mourned her death, but also, the people of the world.

The gates of the formal and stately Buckingham Palace became merely a backdrop for the wreaths, flowers, stuffed animals, notes and other expressions of love and mourning. She stepped out of the palace, lived among the people, loved the people, befriended the people and deeply touched their lives. She was a fairy tale come to life.

But the greatest decent from greatness took place long before Mark Twain wrote *The Prince and the Pauper*. Long before Disney's *Aladdin*. Long before England's great princess.

God came near.

> In the beginning was the Word, and the Word was with God, and the Word was fully God. Now the Word became flesh and took up residence among us. (John 1:1, 14)

> Though he [Jesus] was God, he did not think of equality with God as something to cling to. ⁷Instead, he gave up his divine privileges; he took the humble position of a slave and was born as a human being. (Phil. 2:6-7 NLT)

The greatest fairy tale of all time is reality. The Creator stepped down into creation. The Creator took on the nature of the creature. Eternal God stepped into time. The King of all creation entered into a dirty stable, born of a peasant woman and a simple carpenter. Jesus chose to leave the majesty, glory, perfection and magnificence of heaven. We can't even begin to comprehend the glories of heaven. And Jesus left it to come **here**! For you and me. Unthinkable! This just doesn't happen!

But it did. God did come near. Jesus, the eternal Son of God, became one of us. This is not a fairy tale. This is not the idea of a great novelist. This is truth. This is reality. This is not fiction. This is fact.

But this is more than just fact. If this is only a matter of fact, only a matter of a historical event, then we have not really understood. If our emotions are impacted by the stories of Prince Edward, Princess Jasmine and Princess Diana, then we ought to be touched to the very core of our emotions when we consider the true wonder of majesty among humanity – Jesus.

The beauty, humility, kindness, grace, mercy, and warmth of Princess Diana's work among the world's outcasts tugs at our hearts and moves us to compassion and a desire to impact people like she did. Surely a look at Jesus should move us, inspire us, compel us with a passion to be like Him. Take a look at the real King among the people!

Let me draw the contrasts a little more clearly. On the one hand, you have human royalty humbling themselves to the level of the common man and you admire them. On the other hand, you have the Son of God humbling himself to become a man. What admiration do you have for Him?

On the one hand, you have a princess visiting people in hospitals and orphanages, and you take note of compassion and mercy. On the other hand, you have the perfect, sinless, pure, holy Son of God who actually healed disease and took children into His arms and blessed them.

Do you see the true glory of real compassion and mercy?

You see a princess befriending the citizens of her country and you applaud her, praising her for being approachable and meek. On the other hand, you have the one who existed in unimaginable glory who calls you His *friend*.

Can you contain the applause and praise?

She was human – created, born, lived and died. Just like every other human. And you recognize greatness because she, being royalty, touched the lives of the people.

He is God – Creator. Eternal yet born, lived, died, alive again. Not like any other human. That's true greatness. Let the wonder, and magnificence touch your heart.

You cannot really appreciate the magnificence of these truths if you don't let them sink deep within your meditations and resonate in your heart. So stop for a moment right now and meditate on the glory of God coming to live with us.

This Christmas, please don't let the activities and celebration of a holiday eclipse the awe, the wonder, and the worship of Jesus.

Today, the day we celebrate His birth, just can't pass by without the focus being on Him.

That may be the norm for many.

Please don't let it be the way your day goes today.

Christmas is the celebration
of the birth of our Savior.
Is it?
For you?

JESUS
Messiah

There had never been a more anticipated event in all of history. The coming of Israel's Messiah. The promises were hundreds of years old. With each new prophecy the anticipation built. But as time passed, the hope, at times, was dashed to the rocks. We can't imagine what it must have been like for every person through those many years of waiting. It has been suggested that every pregnant woman would have wondered if they would give birth to the Messiah.

With each conquest by a foreign nation and the tyranny that followed, the passion for freedom grew. And so did their focus on a Messiah who would bring them this freedom.

And so as the birth of Jesus Messiah approached, the anticipation reached its climax. We see it in each new announcement of Jesus' birth and interactions between people who heard these announcements.

When the angel Gabriel told Mary about Jesus' coming birth, he told her, "The Lord God will give him the **throne** of his ancestor David. 33And he will **reign** over Israel forever; his Kingdom will never end!" (Luke 1:32-33)

Gabriel's announcement to Mary is very clear. Jesus Messiah will rule over Israel as the rightful king in the line of David. Jesus' birth was the fulfillment of this Old Testament prophecy/promise. Mary understood this and praised God for it. (Luke 1:50-55)

Mary praised God for His faithfulness to His covenant with Israel, demonstrated by His rescuing Israel from its enemies over and over again. And now, her understanding of what God was doing gave her confidence that God will again come to Israel's aid, bringing victory over their enemies through Messiah.

When John the Baptist was born, Zechariah was filled with the Holy Spirit and declared Jesus to be the mighty Savior from David's line who will save Israel from their enemies, in fulfillment of God's covenant promises. (Luke 1:67-79)

Israel's anticipation of a Messiah who would liberate them from the oppression of Rome was not something they came up with on their own. It was the promise of God to send them a liberating King who would take David's throne.

The problem with their anticipation of Messiah's coming was that it became limited to Messiah coming to be a political liberator who would give them freedom from oppression and would bring in a time of peace and prosperity. And this focus became so limited that they missed the other aspects of the prophecies about Messiah. They missed the part about John the Baptist preparing the way for the Messiah by calling people to repentance from sin and holy living. They missed the part about Messiah leading people to spiritual revival, not just political rescue and prosperity.

Zechariah got it. He didn't just prophecy about Messiah rescuing Israel from their enemies and ruling on David's throne. He saw Messiah's rescue liberating people "so we can serve God without fear, in holiness and righteousness for as long as we live." (Luke 1:74-75)

This problem of the people of Jesus' day continued all through His life. This was a major reason for the crucifixion. The people wanted a Messiah of their making. Really, they just wanted someone to give them political freedom and make their lives better – as they saw fit. They didn't want a Messiah who would tell them how to live or call them to repentance.

Think about it. The crowds praised Jesus as the Messianic King on Sunday but cried for His crucifixion on Friday. Why would crowds of worshipers turn on Jesus so quickly? Maybe because they were a lot like many of us today. We expect God to free us from oppression and give us the freedom of self-rule. We want God to fix or remove anyone who interferes with our comfort and plans. Too often, we want a god that gives us a world where we are free to do as we please without interference from anyone – including God. So, when God doesn't deliver this in our lives, we become disinterested in God – even upset with God for not fixing our world. We don't think God's working for us, so we distance ourselves from God, stop spending time with Him – in His Word, in His church.

We expect God to bless us and make our lives comfortable - especially if we do something for Him. Like Israel, sometimes we just want God to be our benefactor – fix my problems, take care of me, bless me, help me build *my* kingdom.

Jesus did not come to take the throne to establish a kingdom on earth that would give the people blessing and prosperity. God's primary goal is not blessing us with the things of this world. God is all about freeing us from our attachment and focus on the things of this world. God is not all about helping us build our kingdom. God is all about us helping Him build His kingdom.

Many people expect God to give them material and physical blessing. They do things like go to church, give, and serve for the purpose of getting a physical blessing.

We don't want God to mess with our way of life and tell us how to live. The Jews wanted Jesus to be *a* king, but not *my* king. They didn't want Jesus to be the authority they had to honor and obey. The people refused to accept Jesus on His terms – repentance and faith and obedience, following His ways and His leading in life.

Just like the people of Jesus' day, we misinterpret Scripture and misunderstand what it means to follow Jesus. The people didn't get it because they had a mixed-up idea of who the Messiah would be and what He would do. They totally missed the *spiritual* nature of the Messiah's kingdom. They focused only on the things Scripture said about the *physical* kingdom.

We want a Bible that makes us feel good and never tells us we're wrong. I want Jesus to lead me when I want answers about my job, major life decisions, fixing my problems. It doesn't work that way. Following Jesus is not something we can do on our terms . . . if we like it or not. Following Jesus means following Him in everything He says . . . obeying Him in everything He commands.

We don't want God to mess with our religion and tell us performance and ritual aren't enough. We're comfortable with a religion that only asks us to come to church a couple times a month and maybe throw a couple coins in the offering. We're comfortable with a religion that says if our good outweighs our bad, then we're all good. But we don't want God to tell us He expects more of us than that!
So when we come up against the things God says about our motives and our hearts, sometimes we push back.

This Christmas, can you take a few minutes to get honest about all this with yourself – and God?

What role does Jesus play in your life? Why do you seek Him? Are you pretty much in it for the blessings you hope to get? Are you focused on Jesus as the one to fix your life, make you comfortable, provide for you so you can have all the nice things you want in life? What do you pray for? More of what you want, or more of Jesus?

The Son of God, eternally existing in the magnificence and perfection of heaven. came to this earth. He lived a perfect life. Loved people through humble service. He suffered and died on the cross to take the punishment we deserve and pay the penalty for our sins.

He didn't do this so that we can have freedom to do as we please. He didn't do this so we can have comfort, peace, and prosperity here on this earth. He did it so we can come into personal relationship with the God of all creation through Him. He did it to give us so much more than anything we could gain in this world. He may bless us with personal comfort, health, prosperity, and other blessings. But none of these are what He saves us to live for. Let's get it right this Christmas.

JESUS
Wonderful Counselor

For to us a child is born, to us a son is given, and the government will be on his shoulders. And he will be called **Wonderful Counselor**, Mighty God, Everlasting Father, Prince of Peace. (Isaiah 9:6)

Summer camp was a big part of my life growing up. With summer camp came the anticipation of lots of fun activities. Archery, canoeing, sailing, swimming in the lake, and great times with friends. Those were good times. And, of course, there were also Bible lessons and camp counselors. I didn't value those as much, to be honest. Later in life, after I surrendered to the Lord, I became a camp counselor and then a supervisor of counselors. I learned what a hard job it is!

As adults, it often takes us a while to figure out that we don't have all the answers. Oh, we'll say it quickly enough, but then we continue to rely on ourselves for the answers. When we finally decide we need help figuring our mess out, we may turn to counselors. For sure, we want a trained counselor. We want someone who can help. Enter Jesus.

In Isaiah nine, we find four titles for Jesus that teach us a lot about who He is, and how we should relate to Him. The first title is "Wonderful Counselor." The Hebrew word *pala* – wonderful – speaks of something that is beyond human explanation. It is something we would never think of, or fully understand. It's way out there. Amazing. Profound.

The second part of this title of the coming Messiah is counselor. It was used in Hebrew to describe a king giving counsel to his people. Knowledge and wisdom are there in the meaning, along with **governing authority** to give the counsel and make it stick.

As Wonderful Counselor, Messiah provides authoritative counsel we would be wise to follow. But, not just because of the authority behind it, but because it comes from a counselor with extraordinary knowledge and wisdom.

> And the Spirit of the LORD will rest on him [Messiah] -- the Spirit of wisdom and understanding, the Spirit of counsel and might, the Spirit of knowledge and the fear of the LORD. (Isaiah 11:2)

This counsel is beyond what man would ever come up with. In fact, in many cases, it is the direct opposite of what man would come up with. But it is backed by perfect knowledge and divine wisdom.

> Oh, the depth of the riches of the wisdom and knowledge of God! How unsearchable his judgments, and his paths beyond tracing out! 34 Who has known the mind of the Lord? Or who has been his counselor?" (Romans 11:33-34)

This is what Jesus, the Wonderful Counselor brought to life. Paul wrote that in Jesus "are hidden all the treasures of wisdom and knowledge" (Colossians 2:3). And everyone knew it.

> When he taught there in the synagogue, everyone was amazed and said, "Where does he get this wisdom and the power to do miracles?" (Matthew 13:54)

As a camp counselor, you spend time in training, pray, and then pray a bunch more. You pour your heart into the kids, and well, too many of them are like me when I was that age. They don't show any signs that they're listening. It's frustrating, and it can really break your heart.

This same story plays out in pastoral counseling as well. Lots of prayer, study, meditation and other prep goes into meeting with a couple struggling with marital problems. You meet with them and, you believe, the Holy Spirit works through you as you pour out God's Word and your heart. They push back. Not always, but way too many times.

I remember one couple very clearly. I shared with them a verse of Scripture and engaged them in thinking about what the verse means for us practically in relationships. They understood. But then, the push back. "Well, what if she . . ." "What if he . . ." Ok, let's look at the verse again. What does it say? Ok, got it. "But you can't expect me to . . ." No, but God can, and He does.

Sometimes the answer is so simple and clear. But, it's hard to put it into practice. So we push back and determine we can't and won't do it. And that is where we sabotage our own path forward in life. And this doesn't just happen in marital counseling. People push back against biblical counseling in many areas of life. Finances, moral issues, other relationship issues – in each of these and more, we push back against biblical counsel we don't like.

Sometimes we might insist, "I do want Jesus to be my Wonderful Counselor. I wish Jesus would give me direction." We say we want Him to speak to us, to give us His wonderful counsel, but we often forget, **He already has!** Jesus gives His wonderful counsel through the Word of God.

> Your word is a lamp to my feet and a light for my path. (Psalm 119:105)

> All Scripture is inspired by God and is useful to teach us what is true and to make us realize what is wrong in our lives. It corrects us when we are wrong and teaches us to do what is right. (2 Timothy 3:16)

God's Word is wonderful counsel! It **does** show us the right path to take in life. Scripture is powerful and practical. Paul states its practicality in four truths about Scripture. First, it will show what is true, what is right, what is God's wisdom for life. Second, it will show us when we are on the wrong path – the path that leads to our destruction. Third, it will show us how to get back on the correct path of wisdom. Fourth, it will teach us how to stay on the right path. That's helpful, powerful wisdom coming from the Wonderful Counselor, found in the Bible.

God has given us a treasure of principles and wisdom for life in His Word. If I want to make great choices and wise decisions, I have to know God's ways through God's Word. Great choices and wise decisions are always built on the principles of God's Word. God's will for my life will always line up with God's will found in His Word. The Wonderful Counselor has spoken.

> But the Counselor, the Holy Spirit, whom the Father will send in my name, will teach you all things and will remind you of everything I have said to you. (John 14:26)

The Wonderful Counselor *is* speaking through the Holy Spirit who gives us understanding of the Word of God so we can accomplish the will of God in specific life circumstances. If I want to make great choices and wise decisions, I need to be sensitive and responsive to the leading of the Holy Spirit in applying God's Word to life choices. The Wonderful Counselor is speaking.

The Wonderful Counselor has spoken. The Wonderful Counselor is speaking. Are you listening?

"This is what the LORD says - your Redeemer, the Holy One of Israel: 'I am the LORD your God, who teaches you what is best for you, who directs you in the way you should go. If only you had paid attention to my commands, your peace would have been like a river, your righteousness like the waves of the sea.'" (Isaiah 48:17-18)

The queen of Sheba will also stand up against this generation on judgment day and condemn it, for she came from a distant land to hear the wisdom of Solomon. Now someone greater than Solomon is here—but you refuse to listen. (Matthew 12:42)

What will you do? Will you push back and brush the wonderful counsel aside? Will you suffer the consequences of not listening to the Wonderful Counselor?

Are you listening?

JESUS

Mighty God

And he will be called Wonderful Counselor, **Mighty God**,
Everlasting Father, Prince of Peace. (Isaiah 9:6)

It's easy for our view of Jesus to be diminished by the fact that we so
naturally identify with Him as a human being. It's easy to think of Him as
a really, really awesome – even sinless – human. But He is so much
more! Yes, He was truly human, 100% human. But He was, and is, and
always has been "Mighty God."

The word "mighty" comes from the Hebrew word, *gibbor.* The exact
meaning of this word is defined by the context in which it is used. The
root meaning of this word describes a man as a noble, honorable, and
fearless warrior hero.

In this root meaning, we see Jesus as a fearless warrior in battle, the
source of victory who will ultimately gain victory over all evil. Jesus is a
fearless, powerful, and victorious Savior, a divine champion who will
never disappoint. Jesus will never fail to honor His promises to lead us
to ultimate victory.

That. Is. Awesome.

But it doesn't go far enough. When this word is used in relation to God
as it is here in Isaiah 9 of Messiah, it refers to the unlimited power of
God. The reality that Jesus is God is critical to this whole title, "Mighty
God." Without the deity of Jesus, the "mighty" aspect of this title loses
its true significance.

Jesus is God in all His glorious greatness and goodness, the almighty
Creator-God. And so, to fully appreciate what it means that Jesus is
"Mighty God", we must consider what Scripture says about the power

of God. To do that, let me take you on a little journey through stellar science.

You probably didn't know this fun fact: Each second, the sun produces enough energy to run our entire planet for nearly 500,000 years. Each second. Power for the whole planet. For 500,000 years! Is that incredible or what? I can't get my head around that. That's just amazing power!

Now if that blows you away, try this one. Let me tell you about supernovas. At the top of this page, you can see a picture of one by the name of Cassiopeia.

When a supernova explodes, scientists tell us it can outshine an entire galaxy and give off more energy than the sun will for as long as they expect it to exist. That's just one, single supernova giving off as much energy as the sun will ever produce! And astronomers have observed numerous supernovas and continue to track a few hundred every year. I know this is some pretty deep scientific information, but I really hope you're getting the incredible magnitude of this.

All of that power is so astonishing to me. Of course, I can't fully understand it all. In fact, it's actually a bit frightening to me to think of that unimaginable amount of power being unleashed multiple times over in the universe.

But do you know what really, really gets me? It's that God's power makes all that other mind-blowing power – combined—look like a watch battery compared to a nuclear power plant. Or maybe, the more accurate comparison would be to say the total power of all the supernovae that have ever existed is like a watch battery compared to God's power! Let this truth sink in. If all the energy in the world were put together it could not begin to approach the staggering power of God.

This isn't just dumb science fiction or theory either. This is reality. The power of those supernovae is very, very real. And our God created all that power! And He didn't work hard to create it either!

The LORD merely spoke, and the heavens were created. He breathed the word, and all the stars were born. . . . ⁹when he spoke, the world began! It appeared at his command. (Psalm 33:6,9 NLT)

There's a fantastic thought in those verses. Did you catch it? There is more power in the voice – the voice of God – than in all the power of creation combined! God doesn't need to lift a finger to do anything!

Jesus, Mighty God, can handle whatever comes my way. He doesn't have to lift a finger to deliver me from my greatest challenges. All He has to do is speak the word!

> The voice of the LORD hews out flames of fire.
> ⁸The voice of the LORD shakes the wilderness;
> The LORD shakes the wilderness of Kadesh.
> ⁹The voice of the LORD makes the deer to calve
> And strips the forests bare;
> And in His temple everything says, "Glory!"
> ¹⁰The LORD sat as King at the flood; Yes,
> the LORD sits as King forever.
> ¹¹The LORD will give strength to His people;
> The LORD will bless His people with peace.
> (Psalm 29:7-11)

There it is! The mighty, limitless, awesome, and even terrifying power of God becomes a source of personal peace and comfort. Do you see it in verse eleven? The Lord whose voice breaks mighty cedars to splinters, sends out flames of fire, shakes the wilderness, and strips the forests bare will give strength to His people!

It isn't just lifeless fact. It is real. It is personal. It is the power of God at work for you. This is so incredible! Makes me feel like shouting! So I need to stop and ask you, "Is Jesus your Mighty God?" We're not after a robotic answer that is only an intellectual statement of fact and has no life-changing quality or conviction to it. We are chasing after a knowledge of God that impacts life and experience. When I ask who your God is, I'm not just asking about what you say, but how you live. I want you to search deep within your heart and then take a good hard look at how you think and act and how you view life and the challenges you face each day.

Really . . . honestly . . . who is Jesus to you? Is he truly **your** Mighty God? I know you believe in your head that God is limitless in power. I know that you believe that there is nothing beyond His infinite ability. But I am challenging you to confront yourself in your worry, anxiety, and self-reliance, and commit to a fresh, determined resolve to trust in Jesus, your Mighty God in every circumstance of life. God's power is greater than the biggest problem you will ever face! Determine to live out this truth.

As I face the challenges and battles of life, I need to remind myself that I have a heroic, powerful, valiant warrior on my side who guarantees my ultimate victory.

But I'm not experiencing much victory right now. This battle has been going on for a long time. I'm not feeling very victorious. In these times, we need to remember that the ultimate victory is coming and trust our Mighty God in the process of the battles of life.

The faith I need to develop is not just about trusting my "Mighty God" to produce a specific outcome I desire. It must be about trusting Him for the process that leads to **His** wisely designed outcome that is for my highest good and His greatest glory. It may not be the outcome I desire, but it will be the strength to endure and honor Him in the undesirable circumstances of life.

I must remember that my "Mighty God" who is able to lead me to the best end for me, is also my "Wonderful Counselor" who knows the best path to that end. I need to work on trusting Him in the process!

JESUS
Everlasting Father

And he will be called Wonderful Counselor, Mighty God,
Everlasting Father, Prince of Peace. (Isaiah 9:6)

Now here's something that could give you a deep theological rash. "His name will be called Wonderful Counselor, Mighty God, Everlasting Father . . ." Wait, stop. ***Father!?!*** How could Jesus be called father? It seems like we're messing with the trinity here and our traditional theology.

But the problem here is not in our theology. It is in our English translations and lack of understanding of ancient culture and practices. The actual Hebrew word translated "everlasting" or "eternal" actually refers to continuing on into the future, forever. It has no actual reference to the past unless the context specifically indicates it. That only happens two times in the Old Testament. So, everlasting is the better translation. And the title is best translated, "Everlasting Father."

But that does not clear up our confusion with calling Jesus Father. To make sense of that, we need to understand this in light of ancient culture. In Ancient culture the king or ruler of a country could be referred to as the "father" of the country with the idea that this ruler had the authority and responsibility of a family father. These responsibilities were to protect, care for, and provide for his family -- or country. This concept of a ruler being a "father" to the people is used elsewhere by Isaiah (Isiah 22:21) and is found in historical records around the time of Isaiah.

This understanding is also supported by the broader context of this title. As Isaiah describes the coming Messiah, he is thinking about the Messiah ruling over His messianic kingdom.

For to us a child is born, to us a son is given, and the **government will be on his shoulders**. And he will be called Wonderful Counselor, Mighty God, Everlasting Father, Prince of Peace. [7]Of the greatness of his **government** and peace there will be no end. He will **reign** on David's throne and over his **kingdom**, establishing and upholding it with justice and righteousness from that time on and forever. The zeal of the LORD Almighty will accomplish this. (Isaiah 9:6-7)

This whole passage is about the Messiah and His rule as king. It describes who He is and how we will rule. He is a king who gives extraordinary counsel that far exceeds man's best wisdom. He is Mighty God, ruling with honor as the valiant warrior who will be victorious over all evil.

Now, we see Messiah as the king who will rule as the Everlasting Father. Unlike so many harsh, mean and vengeful rulers of that day who oppressed the people, Messiah will come and rule like a father, with kindness, compassion, love, gentleness, serving and building up people.

"Here is my servant, whom I uphold, my chosen one in whom I delight; I will put my Spirit on him, and he will bring justice to the nations. [2]He will not shout or cry out, or raise his voice in the streets. [3]A bruised reed he will not break, and a smoldering wick he will not snuff out. In faithfulness he will bring forth justice. (Isaiah 42:1-3)

Yes, Messiah would be passionate about righteousness and justice. But Isaiah previews the ministry of Messiah saying He will seek righteousness and justice primarily through love and compassion. He wouldn't go around shouting a screaming at people, telling them how evil they were (v. 2). He would gently lead them to recognize their sin and embrace repentance. He would lift up those who had experienced abuse and oppression (v.3).

And as we look at Jesus' ministry, that is what we see. We see Jesus as the gentle Messiah-King, demonstrated in who He associated with. It was almost always common ordinary people, and often outcasts and marginalized people. Diseased people, sinners, Samaritans. He had no barriers, no prejudices. Always patient. Always gentle. Always meeting people where they were in their place of need. The only time Jesus became confrontational was when He faced spiritual pride and rebellion.

His compassion for hurting people was evident so many times in His life. He healed. He fed. He stopped to pay attention. Even when He was in the middle of something, He saw the needy and responded.

> When he saw the crowds, he had compassion on them because they were confused and helpless, like sheep without a shepherd. (Matthew 9:36)

> Jesus saw the huge crowd as he stepped from the boat, and he had compassion on them and healed their sick. (Matthew 14:14)

> Moved with compassion, Jesus reached out and touched him. "I am willing," he said. "Be healed!" [42]Instantly the leprosy disappeared, and the man was healed. (Mark 1:41-42)

Some humbling questions come to my mind when I think about all this:
- Am I harsh or demanding in my leadership or position of authority?
- Do I see the needy or am I too caught up in my own agenda?
- Am I compassionate, patient, and loving?
- Do I lift people up with gentle care and encouragement?
- Am I harsh in speaking the truth and confronting people?

There's another side to this. It is the side of the hurting, weak, and discouraged. What can we take away from this when we find ourselves dragging around the pain of mistreatment, abusive people, and being in a dark place in life?

> Then Jesus said, "Come to me, all of you who are weary and carry heavy burdens, and I will give you rest. [29]Take my yoke upon you. Let me teach you, because I am humble and gentle at

heart, and you will find rest for your souls. [30]For my yoke is easy to bear, and the burden I give you is light." (Matthew 11:28-30)

Those of us who know little about farming may need to get clued in on yokes to understand what Jesus was saying here. A yoke is a wooden bar that connects two animals together, usually donkeys or oxen, that is then connected to a plow. Jesus pictures two types of yokes. One that is a great burden to bear, and one that is easier.

There were those of Jesus' day – as there are today – who were overburdened with the rules and requirements of religious leaders. It's like being yoked to an overbearing ox. This yoke involves the endless efforts to get it right and measure up, to be considered the real deal. If you don't measure up, you are treated as inferior, talked about, and avoided.

On the other hand, there is the yoke Jesus offers. He offers rest from the heavy burden. His teaching is gentle, patient, filled with grace and mercy. It is **always** what is for our greatest good. He doesn't lay a heavy burden on us – **never** more than necessary. He will lead us to see how we need to repent, change, and grow, for sure. But we can go to Him and be confident he won't bully us around or throw the book at us in a fit of anger.

This is similar to the contrast of the harsh, tyrannical king with the gentleness of our Messiah-King who governs like a gentle, loving father. Jesus' life and ministry prove Him to be our Everlasting Father, full of compassion, tender care, and gentle leadership.

Wherever you are at, you don't need to run from Jesus. You don't need to fear that He will come at you with the belt in a fit of rage. You can run to Him, knowing that He will embrace you like a loving father. Know that whatever you are asked to do, wherever you are asked to go, you are being led by the fatherly love of Jesus.

JESUS
Prince of Peace

And he will be called Wonderful Counselor, Mighty God, Everlasting Father, **Prince of Peace**. (Isaiah 9:6)

We live in a world filled with conflict and war. We will often stay somewhat isolated from the international conflict and war and even isolated from the conflict and crime all around us as we focus on our own lives. But we have our own personal conflicts with others and our own personal, internal conflicts.

We too often live in turmoil. Unsettled. And we want to turn to God for help, but sometimes, we're not sure we have peace with Him either. We blow it, we fail, we fall into the same sin *–again*. And we don't have a sense of peace with God.

But Christmas is a celebration of peace! One of the titles of Jesus Messiah is "Prince of Peace". The people of Isaiah would understand this to mean that the Messiah would be the one to bring peace, lead peace, oversee and maintain peace. While the rulers of the earth are often initiating conflict and endless wars, Messiah will bring peace.

In the Jewish understanding, peace meant freedom from conflict, but it also meant much more. *Shalom* includes harmony, wholeness, stability, and well-being. And it wasn't just a feeling, it was a way of living that was pursued. This is what Messiah will ultimately bring to reality. And this is what the angel announced the night Jesus-Messiah was born.

> Suddenly, the angel was joined by a vast host of others-- the armies of heaven-- praising God and saying, ¹⁴"Glory to God in highest heaven, and peace on earth to those with whom God is pleased." (Luke 2:13-14)

The birth of Jesus is the birth of peace that will touch every fiber of human existence. It begins a process that will lead to genuine peace. Peace with God. Peace within ourselves. Peace with others in our lives. Peace in the world.

The full realization of this peace will only come in Messiah's future kingdom, but there is so much peace we can experience now because Jesus in our Prince of Peace. For His peace to win out in our lives, the cause of conflict, anxiety, fear, and despair must be defeated. Sin must be dealt with. Our broken relationship with God must be dealt with. And that is exactly what our Messiah does.

We are all sinners (Romans 3:23) Every single one of us were hopelessly, helplessly dead in our sins (Ephesians 2:1). No one needs Jesus more or less than anyone else! No one.

> But now in Christ Jesus you who once were *far away* have been brought near through the blood of Christ. [14]For *he himself is our peace*, who has made the two one and has destroyed the barrier, the dividing wall of hostility, [15]by abolishing in his flesh the law with its commandments and regulations. His purpose was to create in himself one new man out of the two, thus making *peace*, [16]and in this one body to reconcile both of them to God through the cross, by which he put to death their hostility. [17]He came and preached *peace* to you who were far away and peace to those who were near. (Ephesians 2:13-17)

Our religious background makes no difference. It never gives anyone a "one up" on anyone else. Whether we start out in total rejection of God, unsure about God, or believing there is a God – yes, even if we believed in the existence of Jesus – it makes no difference whatsoever. Dead in sin is dead in sin. Without faith in Christ we are still dead in our sins, under God's wrath, and in need of peace with God.

Our social or economic status makes no difference either. Our ethnicity means nothing. Neither have any value in saving us. No one is exempt from the need of a Savior and no one is too far gone for the Savior! Jesus came to give us life, forgiveness, and peace with God as a gracious gift. Jesus came to be our peace and to "preach peace". Jesus came to make a way to peace with God for everyone by grace through faith.

> Therefore, since **we have been made right in God's sight by faith**, **we have peace with God** because of what Jesus Christ our Lord has done for us. [2]Because of our faith, Christ has brought us into this place of undeserved privilege where we now stand, and we confidently and joyfully look forward to sharing God's glory. (Romans 5:1-2)

Peace with God is not built on getting it all right, but on getting right with God through faith in Jesus alone. And that faith also brings us to the place of being at peace with God.

> So now there is no condemnation for those who belong to Christ Jesus. (Romans 8:1)

> Who dares accuse us whom God has chosen for his own? No one-- for God himself has given us right standing with himself. [34]Who then will condemn us? No one-- for Christ Jesus died for us and was raised to life for us, and he is sitting in the place of honor at God's right hand, pleading for us. (Romans 8:33-34)

Satan is our accuser. But the verdict has already been handed down in the courtroom of heaven for those who have placed their faith in Christ. There is no condemnation! We are forgiven. The debt has been paid. The accuser is silenced! Don't listen to the lies of Satan! Don't dishonor the grace of God by drowning in guilt and avoiding God. Don't beat yourself up over unknown sin, unintentional mistakes and inabilities. Celebrate God's forgiveness and restoration, and His promise to take your failures and turn them around for good in your life. Embrace by faith the truth that you have peace with God through Christ and discover peace within, even when Satan attacks.

The Prince of Peace provides all we need to have peace with God. Knowing that He is truly on our side, looking out for our best and our inner sense of well-being can give us peace when life's challenges rock our foundation. Peace is found when we trust Him, taking Him at His word that He is working for us, not against us.

You will keep in perfect peace all who trust in you, all whose thoughts are fixed on you! ⁴Trust in the LORD always, for the LORD GOD is the eternal Rock. (Isaiah 26:3-4)

There are two essentials for peace in these verses: focus and trust. God will give us peace when we choose to trust Him. No, this is not easy, but the truth must prevail in our hearts and minds. God can be trusted with everything in our lives – every detail, no matter how small or big! So, we must focus on God, the truth of His Word, and His promises to us. We can focus on what brings us turmoil, anxiety and fear, or we can focus on God and find peace. Focus and trust!

But what about the conflict in our lives and in the world all around us? The truth is, we will always conflict in our lives and in the world until Jesus establishes His kingdom. He told us we would have conflict with others. Some is due to our own sinful attitudes and behaviors in our relationships. When this is true, we need to repent of and seek forgiveness. We need to get back to adorning the gospel. We need to do all we can to assure that conflict is not due to our attitudes or actions. But there will be times when we will face conflict because of our relationship with Christ. He told us this would happen (John 15:18-21). In these situations, we need to rest in our peace with God, leave the relationship in His sovereign hands, and continue to honor Him in the relationship. Trust the Prince of Peace.

Peace can be ours because Jesus-Messiah is our Prince of Peace.

JESUS

Victorious

New Year's Eve! We've made it through another year and stand on the brink of a new one. It's a time of looking back over the past year, evaluating, maybe learning from mistakes. And it's a time for looking to the future. Maybe making some resolutions? (Is that still a thing?)

You could say we are in the "in between". The past year is going into the books, and a new chapter is open to a blank page. Did you ever realize that all of our lives fit into the great in between?

Jesus has won the victory! In Christ, Jesus' victory is our victory! But we exist in between the cross and the kingdom. What does that mean? It means that Jesus has finished securing the victory but has not yet established all the results of that victory.

What we find in Scripture – what we see when we look at who we are in Christ – is that His victory over our greatest enemies is our victory. In Christ, we are victorious.

This does not mean we have victory the way we might like to define it. This does not mean we have victory in the timing we would like it. Some say or imply that life for the believer should be one that is free from challenges, financial difficulties, illness, and relationship conflict. But this is not what Scripture teaches. This is not the victory Jesus promises **in this life**.

Yes, in Christ we are guaranteed victory in *every* area that has been negatively impacted by sin and the curse. But many aspects of this victory are the *future* hope of the believer, not a promise of God for the present. We live in between the "already" and the "not yet". Paul walks us through this reality for us, and the rest of creation. He says there are aspects of the victory that Christ secured that all creation, including us, are still waiting for.

> For the creation was subjected to futility-- not willingly, but because of Him who subjected it-- in the hope [21]that the creation itself will also be set free from the bondage of corruption into the glorious freedom of God's children. [22]For we know that the whole creation has been groaning together with labor pains until now. [23]And not only that, but we ourselves who have the Spirit as the firstfruits-- we also groan within ourselves, eagerly waiting for adoption, the redemption of our bodies. [24]Now in this hope we were saved, yet hope that is seen is not hope, because who hopes for what he sees? [25]But if we hope for what we do not see, we eagerly wait for it with patience. (Romans 8:20-25)

Paul is describing for us a tension that exists for every believer. The tension between the "already" and the "not yet" – the in between. There is so much that was accomplished by the work of Christ on the cross. Some of that is part of what we can experience already. But much of what Christ accomplished is to be fully realized in the future. It is part of the "not yet".

Paul says creation is groaning like a woman in labor because of the curse. What is often considered the worst pain of human life? Child birth. But what does it produce? New life! That is our hope, for we also groan within ourselves – we aren't exempt from this groaning experienced by all of creation. One of the things we groan about a lot is these frail bodies we live in. Paul is telling us that this complete victory over the groaning of this life is our future, but absolutely guaranteed hope – guaranteed by the indwelling Spirit. But it not our present reality.

Our Victory is in Christ! Already, we have received victory over the penalty of sin, victory over the power of sin, relationship with God, grace to honor God in relationships, God's provision for all our needs, and so much more.

But there is also our "not yet" victory that is promised to come in the future. Victory over the presence of sin, the complete defeat and eradication of sin and all evil, freedom from sickness and weak physical bodies, conflict-free relationships of perfect love, victory over death, spending eternity in heaven, complete reversal of all the effects of the fall of man, complete restoration of the glory of man created in the image of God. All of this is part of our victory in Jesus.

No longer will there be a curse upon anything. For the throne of God and of the Lamb will be there, and his servants will worship him. (Revelation 22:3)

What a glorious victory! Complete and permanent victory! Can't wait!

But how do I know I'll reach? How do I know I won't blow it? What about losing my salvation? Is "once saved, always saved" really true? Can I really know I will reach this ultimate victory – without a doubt? Let's let Scripture answer those questions. What does Scripture say about our victory? What does Scripture say about our security in Christ?

For those God foreknew he also predestined to be conformed to the likeness of his Son, that he might be the firstborn among many brothers. [30]And those he predestined, he also called; those he called, he also justified; those he justified, he also glorified. (Romans 8:29-30)

Now it is God who makes both us and you stand firm in Christ. He anointed us,[22]set his seal of ownership on us, and put his Spirit in our hearts as a deposit, *guaranteeing* what is to come. (2 Corinthians 1:21-22)
And when you believed in Christ, he identified you as his own by giving you the Holy Spirit, whom he promised long ago. [14]The Spirit is God's guarantee that he will give us the inheritance he promised and that he has purchased us to be his own people. He did this so we would praise and glorify him. (Ephesians 1:13-14)

Now may the God of peace make you holy in every way, and may your whole spirit and soul and body be kept blameless until our Lord Jesus Christ comes again. 24God will make this happen, for he who calls you is faithful. (1 Thessalonians 5:23-24)

God's declared plan for every believer is to make them like Jesus. The future reality of the believer's perfection is a done deal in the plan of God. God decrees and declares what is not yet a reality in time as being already done! There is no maybe here. There is no – it all depends on how we do. He determined that those who put their faith in Christ would ultimately be perfected in Christ. He then called them to himself and declared them to be right with Him. Done deal. But that's not all. He also declares that the process of our growth in Christlikeness is fully completed and our actual perfection is already established as an undisputed reality in heaven.

God declares that a believer is right before Him based on their faith in Christ – no one or no thing in all creation can change this declaration. God has promised and guaranteed our future in heaven by giving us the Holy Spirit forever. If you have genuinely placed your faith in Christ for your salvation and don't make it to heaven, if won't be because you have failed, it will be because God has failed and broken His promise. That can't happen!

> **In Christ, the victories of Jesus on the cross**
> **become my victories.**
> **Some are still to be realized,**
> **but all are guaranteed!**

The seventh angel sounded his trumpet, and there were loud voices in heaven, which said: "The kingdom of the world has become the kingdom of our Lord and of his Messiah, and he will reign for ever and ever." (Revelation 11:15)

Also available by Christopher Berner:

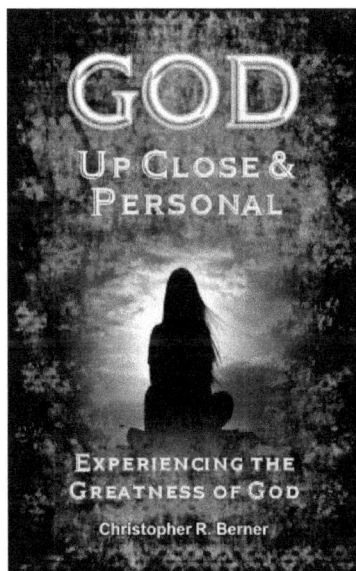

This is a book that will engulf you in amazing truths about the greatness of God. It is specifically designed to accurately present theological truths in a way that is easily understood, engaging, and very practical. Ultimately, that is what this book is all about — transformed lives characterized by peace, confidence, and joy in honoring the greatness of God.

FIND IT AT:

amazon.com.